A HUMAN RESOURCES FRAMEWORK FOR THE PUBLIC SECTOR

A HUMAN RESOURCES FRAMEWORK FOR THE PUBLIC SECTOR

Dixon E. Southworth

////
MANAGEMENTCONCEPTS

ɪɪɪ
MANAGEMENTCONCEPTS
8230 Leesburg Pike, Suite 800
Vienna, VA 22182
(703) 790-9595
Fax: (703) 790-1371
www.managementconcepts.com

Library of Congress Cataloging-in-Publication Data

Southworth, Dixon.
  A human resources framework for the public sector / Dixon Southworth.
    p. cm.
  ISBN 978-1-56726-238-4
1. Personnel management—United States. 2. Civil service—United States—
Personnel management. 3. Human capital—United States. I. Title.
HF5549.2.U5S68 2009
352.60973—dc22

                                                        2008054771

Printed in the United States of America

10   9   8   7   6   5   4   3   2   1

About the Author

Dixon Southworth, MPA, is a consultant for the New York State Comptroller in the Office of Human Resources, where he is developing effectiveness and efficiency measures and measurement instruments for HR programs and services. He recently retired from the New York State Department of Civil Service, where he was a leader in the use and development of performance assessments for civil service examinations. He regularly applies to his work many of the lessons from the Work Performance Framework presented in the book. He received an MPA from Sage Graduate School in Albany in 1995.

To my wife, Linore

Contents

Preface

want to introduce you to a whole new way of looking at human resources—through the lens of a theoretical framework. There is no
shortage of theories about how people achieve success. Some authors
have bonded several theories together, but no one has explained all
human resource (HR) theories. That is the task I have undertaken—to
build a Work Performance Framework (WPF) that unites all the many
valuable theories about work, achievement, success, joy, failure, pain,
isolation, and even generosity and mercy.

The WPF provides information about the many legitimate reasons
that people succeed. The framework is geared toward both people who
naturally do very well in their jobs and those who unknowingly violate
their organization's unwritten rules or taboos and find themselves in an
intolerable state—dispirited by sadness, stress, disorientation, boredom,
fatigue, or disenfranchisement. The WPF will help everyone better understand themselves in a complex work environment, leading to greater
professional success.

The framework is also intended to help HR professionals who oversee
recruitment, development, retention, and labor relations programs, as
well as people who mentor coworkers. Finally, the WPF should prove to

be of great value to academics researching HR management and looking for a new, fresh perspective.

I have developed the WPF for use in the public sector, because this is where I have worked and is what I know best. While organizations in the private sector have more freedom to dictate terms of employment, they are also vulnerable to market forces that can jeopardize their business. With increasing demands for continuous improvement and higher service expectations, the time is ripe for a comprehensive framework for work performance.

The book contains an introductory chapter, three parts, and a concluding chapter. The book aligns with the major facets of the WPF—HR theory, programs, strategic objectives, and research. Chapters 2–8 each include background information on the WPF, a selected literature review, a list of relevant HR programs along with several key measurements and important issues for future research. At the conclusion of each part, I apply the relevant lessons to answer the question, What makes a good worker?

As an introduction, Chapter 1 discusses public administration theory and HR theory and follows with a summary of the contents of the WPF. The chapter concludes by connecting the WPF to strategic workforce planning. Part 1 includes Chapter 2, which describes people as human resources at the stage before they have been fully prepared to work, and Chapter 3, which defines the enablers that prepare people to carry out their work responsibilities. These are the parts of the WPF that precede actual work performance—i.e., the antecedents to work performance.

Part 2 presents work inputs, work processes, and work outputs as the actual components of work performance according to general systems theory. Chapter 4 presents people as work inputs in terms of their competencies, work effort, and power to act. Chapter 5 addresses three sets of work processes—work production, work behaviors, and work improvements and innovations—and Chapter 6 presents work outputs—services, interpersonal communications, and work improvements and innovations.

Part 3 presents the aftereffects of work performance—the outcomes and impacts. Chapter 7 presents program outcomes and people outcomes, and it discusses performance measurements used to evaluate program and worker effectiveness. Chapter 8 presents impacts as the response to work results by workers, customers, or other interested stakeholders. Reponses come in the form of emotions, attitudes, well-being, understanding, and decision-making.

The last chapter summarizes the book and provides concluding comments. The chapter presents two performance dashboards—one HR managers can use to track the performance of their programs and services and one for efficiently reporting program performance. Then, applying the book's lessons, I revisit the question, What makes a good worker? The chapter concludes with a final look at pressing issues for contemporary HR management and opportunities for important research.

Dixon Southworth
Troy, New York

Acknowledgments

want to acknowledge the help from the staff of Management Concepts—Myra Strauss, Courtney Chiaparas, Lena Johnson, and Jared Stearns, and the remarkable editing assistance of Peter Whitten.

PART 1

The Antecedents to Work

An Introduction to the Work Performance Framework

This opening chapter introduces the Work Performance Framework (WPF) as a theoretical construct for work performance in public service. The framework merges human resource (HR) management theories, concepts, and concerns with public administration theories, concepts, and concerns. The WPF is a tool for HR managers and public administrators to use to manage work performance, for public-sector workers to understand and manage their individual and aggregate development and performance, for academics to provide instruction on public-sector work performance, and for researchers to identify new topics and lines of inquiry to explore.

THE THEORETICAL FOUNDATION OF THE WORK PERFORMANCE FRAMEWORK

The WPF is built upon recent literature on public administration theory and HR management theory. While the following literature review does not account for all pertinent theoretical research and discussion in the areas of HR management and public administration, these works were instrumental in the construction of the WPF.

Public Administration Theories

We need a comprehensive theoretical framework to better understand the profession of public administration. If there have been shortcomings in the search for such a framework, it is not for lack of trying. A vast number of books, journals, papers, and conference proceedings abound with discussions, frameworks, formulas, data, statistical analyses, and case studies. Nonetheless, there is still little agreement about what public programs are supposed to accomplish, and there is no universally acknowledged theoretical framework.

R. D. Behn (1995) proposed that scholars in public management entertain big questions, much like those in science. Comparing the "science" of public administration to physics, where questions like the origin of the universe led to the big bang theory, he notes that scientists do not start with data or methods; they begin with questions. Once a big question has been set, the data and methods are developed to achieve the goal. Behn's three big questions for the field of public administration ask how to manage public programs without micromanaging, how to motivate public-sector workers to achieve public purposes, and how to measure agency achievements in a way that leads to greater success. A theoretical framework on work performance would be extremely helpful in addressing Behn's three big questions.

J. C. N. Raadschelders (1999) documented the need for a comprehensive theory of public administration, explaining that the field suffers from identity confusion due to existential and academic crises. He explains that public administration's existential problem stems from the need to separate itself as an independent discipline apart from political science, economics, and business administration. The academic problems, in his view, stem from epistemological questions that must be addressed by applying organizational theories to public organizations, relating theories of human action to the practice of governing, and addressing the extent to which our knowledge of public administration is scientific. Although he does not take on these challenges himself, Raadschelders does present a diagram of public administration as a body of knowledge, cataloging top-ics of discussion under four quadrants (what, who, why, and how) that are the foundation of the general question: what is public administration?

In *The Spirit of Public Administration* (1997), H. George Frederickson argues there should be three pillars of public administration theory—efficiency, economy, and social equity. In positing a compound theory of social equity, Frederickson uses the terms *fairness, justice,* and *equity* interchangeably, where the ultimate goal of social equity is a more equal distribution of opportunities, costs, and benefits. The basis for this activ-ity is that public administrators should be good citizens who benevolently oversee public programs and actively seek to help the less fortunate.

At the 2001 national conference of the American Society for Public Administration (ASPA), this author presented a theoretical framework for public programs. The framework for public programs, which has been incorporated into the WPF, aligns with Frederickson's three pillars for public administration but includes some subtle differences.

The framework for public programs begins with the central premise that public programs must follow one ethical rule: neither provide nor charge for unnecessary services. This premise is analogous to the "invis-ible hand" that ensures efficiency in free enterprise markets. And it leads to the fundamental question: what is the purpose of public programs? Two fundamental purposes of public programs are (1) public programs must provide *important services* that should not and cannot be provided by private businesses, and (2) government is responsible for advancing *social justice.*

The framework for public programs identifies three public program *service* components: (1) prevent or solve societal problems; (2) provide care and compassion; and (3) through the distribution of information and other resources, enable people to solve their own problems.

The framework also proposes four *social justice* components of public programs: (1) equitable laws and procedures that create a level playing field on which people who are motivated to do their best can enjoy substantial individual rewards; (2) generous distribution of our nation's wealth to all citizens, especially the most needy; (3) due process procedures that provide a mechanism for citizen dissent; and (4) a social contract that holds people accountable for being responsible citizens and for helping themselves to the fullest extent possible when aided by public programs.

The intended impact of these public programs is to advance the belief among our citizens that (1) public programs provide important value; (2) the programs are fiscally responsible; (3) the programs balance individual rights and benefits against rights and benefits for all; and (4) because of these programs, our government is good. Thus, we have constructed a working definition of goodness, so "good" public programs are efficient, effective, and fair. (By extension, the "good" public-sector worker is also efficient, effective, and fair.)

Finally, the framework for public programs posits that the desired sustainable result of public programs is *social harmony.*

Human Resource Management Theories

S. E. Jackson and R. S. Schuler (1995) identify a number of contemporary theories that aid an understanding of HR management within the context of the organization. The authors describe the role-behavior perspective, institutional theory, resource-dependent theory, human capital theory, transaction costs theory, agency theory, resource-based theory, and general systems theory. These theories range from evaluating the cost and value of HR management to identifying the interpersonal and social systems that occur in organizations, which workers must understand in order to maneuver effectively. Wright and Snell's management model

(1991) uses general systems theory. Skills and abilities are presented as inputs, employee behaviors are presented as throughputs, and employee satisfaction and performance are outputs.

H. P. Hatry (2001) describes an adapted United Way model for human services programs in which program outcomes encompass "new knowledge," "increased skills," and "changed attitudes or values," which lead to "modified behaviors," which in turn lead to "improved conditions" or "altered states."

Other HR management systems theories add aptitudes and personality traits as inputs in addition to knowledge, skills, and abilities (KSAs) and add work duties, work activities, and tasks as processes in addition to work behaviors.

By incorporating many of the HR management topics discussed by Hatry and by Wright and Snell, the WPF adopts general systems theory as the basis for constructing a comprehensive theoretical framework for HR management. By addressing the public administration topics presented by Behn, Raadschelders, and Frederickson, as well as this author's line of inquiry into public programs, the WPF merges HR management theory with general public administration theory.

OVERVIEW OF THE WORK PERFORMANCE FRAMEWORK

The WPF as a theoretical framework for work performance in public service contains three parts. The first part, consisting of human resources and enablers, addresses the antecedents to work performance, which include raw human resources and the enablers that transform these raw human resources into work inputs. The second part, consisting of work inputs, work processes, and work outputs, addresses actual work performance in a public-sector setting. The third and final part, consisting of outcomes and impacts, addresses the aftereffects of work performance, including public program benefits, HR outcomes, and the impacts of work performance and public programs on workers and other stakeholders. Table 1-1 presents an overview of the WPF.

TABLE 1-1 Work Performance Framework

Human Resources	Enablers	Work Inputs	Work Processes	Work Outputs	Outcomes	Impacts
Mental Ability General mental ability Personality	Education and Training Experience	Competencies Knowledge Skills Abilities	Work Production Direct services Administration Infrastructure Support	Services	Program Outcomes Program benefits Unintended consequences	Emotional Feelings
Physical Ability Fitness Health	Associations Healthy Living	Effort Intention Energy	Work Behaviors	Interpersonal Communication	Human Resource Outcomes Rewards Punishments Obligations Adversities	Psychological Attitudes Judgments Intellectual Reasoning Beliefs
Socioeconomic Conditions Social Financial	Special Programs	Power Authority Resources Influence	Work Improvements and Innovations	New or Improved Systems and Outputs	Evaluation Outcomes Performance measurements Assessments of fairness	Spiritual Well-being

Human Resources and Enablers

In the WPF, human resources are identified as potential abilities; they are differentiated from *applied* abilities, including competencies or KSAs, which are presented as inputs. Potential abilities pass through an enabling process and become applied abilities at the time work is performed. Human resources and enablers, presented in Figure 1-1, precede inputs and are not a part of general systems theory.

FIGURE 1-1 Work Performance Framework—Human Resources and Enablers

Human Resources	Enablers
Mental Ability General Mental Ability Personality	Education and Training Experience Associations
Physical Ability Fitness Health	Healthy Living
Socioeconomic Conditions Social Financial	Special Programs

Human Resources

People begin their quest for achievement with certain mental abilities, physical abilities, and socioeconomic conditions. These resources help to determine the training and development opportunities that are accessible to them, and ultimately which ones they select. These opportunities enhance their prospects for employment and career success. For example, a person with strong mathematical abilities might choose to study engineering and subsequently enter the workforce as an engineer armed with professional engineering KSAs.

Mental abilities are the capacity or capability to perform certain mental activities and include general mental ability represented as g, personality, aptitudes, talents, wisdom, creativity, and charisma. While these abilities are not job-ready, people with greater mental abilities are more likely to learn and understand information presented through education or training, or from on-the-job experience. General mental ability, or g, is considered one of the most reliable predictors of job performance. Nonetheless, it is far from a perfect predictor.

Physical abilities are included as a resource primarily to address effort as a factor of work performance. High performers not only have the mental capacity to deal with complex work situations; they must also have the energy to remain positive and effective under the adverse conditions of long workdays, strained relationships, in-fighting, shortened deadlines, and failing ventures. To offset the possibility that physical ability might be given too much importance in hiring, the Americans with Disabilities Act affords certain protections to people with physical or mental disabilities from employers who would discriminate against a disabled person.

While there is a legitimate interest in hiring energetic people, employers cannot leap to the conclusion on face value alone that a person with a disability necessarily has a low energy threshold or work limitation. Physical ability requirements are also important for security-related positions. Police officers and firefighters, for example, must use their physical abilities to save lives.

Socioeconomic conditions are influential in regard to work performance and likelihood of success. Wealthy people can afford to buy opportunities by, for example, living in the better school districts with better teachers and attending the expensive and exclusive colleges and universities with top-ranked faculty, enormous resources, and networked employment opportunities. Meanwhile, those with moderate or low incomes are often denied these advantages, live in the poorer school districts with fewer resources, and attend technical schools or state-operated colleges or universities, or they have no advanced education at all. Although the advantages of wealth do not absolutely predict individual outcomes, they clearly affect the odds.

In the public sector, helping the underprivileged is especially important. Frederickson defines the goal in terms of social equity, i.e., redistributing wealth to the needy. While some people may take a very conservative view of the government's role in redistributing wealth, it is clear that helping the needy is an ideal embraced by our society as a whole, so the issue of socioeconomic conditions must be addressed within the WPF.

Enablers

The enablers described in the WPF complete the transition of human resources (mental abilities, physical abilities, and socioeconomic conditions) to work inputs (competencies, effort, and power). How does a mental ability become a competency? How does physical ability become effort? How do we help underprivileged people become valued employees? The enablers do it, and they are well known—education, training, experience, exercise, healthy living, and special assistance for those who need it.

Education, in particular higher education, addresses the inputs of professional and technical competencies to enable a person to become, say, a computer analyst, engineer, teacher, lawyer, doctor, or registered professional nurse. At the community college level, a person might become a technical expert such as a plumber, automotive technician, electrician, or licensed practical nurse, while four-year college and graduate-level programs tend to reflect professional-level jobs. Educational programs in public or business administration are available to obtain competencies in management and administration.

Training programs often address competencies related to staff supervision and operational information on pertinent laws, rules, regulations, policies, and procedures. Training programs may also target competencies related to interpersonal relationships, oral presentation, special computer software used by an organization, and customer-service procedures and techniques.

Experience can be gained directly through appointments and promotions, or indirectly through special assignments, internships, or even volunteer work. Such experience can be valuable in developing interpersonal skills and influencing techniques in a work environment, delegating work to others and monitoring their performance, and managing workload. A vital part of on-the-job experience is guidance through mentoring and coaching, which can help maximize the likelihood of a successful work opportunity.

Exercise and healthy living programs are often recognized by the organization as popular with employees and beneficial in reducing employee sick days, but the primary benefit is to increase energy, strength, and stamina to help workers withstand high work demands.

Special assistance includes affirmative action programs that provide employment opportunities to women, minority group members, and disabled workers to help them succeed and advance in the organization. To avoid accusations of reverse discrimination, individuals often targeted for special assistance include the needy population or those people who are socially or economically disadvantaged. An employee assistance program (EAP) in an organization helps employees with special problems navigate through their difficulties without negatively affecting their work performance.

Work Inputs, Processes, and Outputs

Work inputs, processes, and outputs are classic elements of general systems theory; they are the center of the WPF. Figure 1-2 presents inputs, processes, and outputs in the WPF.

FIGURE 1-2 Work Performance Framework—Work Inputs, Processes, and Outputs

Work Inputs	Work Processes	Work Outputs
Competencies Knowledge Skills Abilities	Work Production Direct services Administration Infrastructure Support	Services
Effort Intention Energy	Work Behaviors	Interpersonal Communication
Power Authority Resources Influence	Work Improvements and Innovations	New or Improved Systems and Outputs

Work Inputs

People as inputs are presented as a combination of competencies, effort, and power. Within the WPF, competencies are identified as applied abilities once actual work is performed, and are differentiated from potential abilities, which, as explained earlier, go through an enabling process.

Traditional civil service examinations concentrate on competencies, often identified as KSAs. Personal attributes are also sometimes presented as inputs and evaluated by special screening devices such as personality tests, psychological tests, and integrity tests. Competencies are included in the WPF as an input, although they too can go through an enabling process.

For the purpose of developing civil service examinations, KSAs can be broken down into several general categories:

- Professional or technical

- Operational

- Administrative, managerial, and/or supervisory

- Writing and computation

- Computer

- Reasoning and decision-making

- Oral presentation

- Customer service and interpersonal relationships.

These categories are also helpful when linking duties to KSAs during job analysis.

The WPF also includes two other elements—effort and power—as input variables. The reasoning is that a person might have the competence to work, but might not put in the effort. Or a person might properly apply her competence to a work assignment with sufficient effort, but if she is not empowered to act, the assignment may be blocked from completion. Sometimes a person attempts to act anyway by assuming the authority to act, thus having de facto power. When things work out well, this may be a feather in our cap, but if things go wrong, we can be subject to punishment for misconduct.

Effort can be broken down into two categories: intention and energy. There are many HR theories related to employee intentions, such as motivation and self-efficacy. But good intentions are not enough; one must also have the energy, i.e., the strength and stamina for a demanding work schedule. Effort includes both physical and mental energy, particularly when work is performed under adverse conditions. Often, adversities— such as personality conflicts, abbreviated deadlines, long days, or dangerous situations—require a great deal of strength and stamina, and often people decline promotions because they are not willing to take on the burden of these adversities.

Power is divided into three categories: authority, resources, and influence. Authority includes the permission that can come with job title, work duties, span of control, special assignments, and special projects. Power also includes access to the financial, capital, or staff resources needed to complete the work. Influence refers to the capacity to influence others.

While a person may have access to needed resources and jurisdiction over decision-making, to wield power effectively one must be able to influence others to act according to plan. Competencies aligned with influence include interpersonal skills, communication skills, and sound analysis and decision-making skills. These competencies are often evaluated by oral tests and assessment centers. Effort can also be a key part of influencing others. Lethargic leaders are unlikely to inspire or influence staff in a positive way.

Work Processes and Work Outputs

Work processes are the actions that people go through to produce work outputs. To understand and appreciate the processes, one must also understand the outputs. In the WPF, processes fall into three areas: (1) production, (2) behaviors, and (3) improvements and innovations. Production outputs include products, services, and information, although in the public service most outputs are services or information pertaining to the services. Work processes aligned with production include the normal work duties, activities, and tasks that appear in a job description. Performance standards often relate to product or service quality, efficiency, and reliability.

Work behaviors have often been linked with work activities, and some theorists use the two terms interchangeably. The WPF separates these two processes and presents a separate output—interpersonal communication—for work behaviors. Performance standards for interpersonal communication most closely align with trust and affiliation. Some confusion, which is addressed later in the book, arises from the fact that service is a production outcome, and trust and affiliation are important aspects of service quality.

Work processes related to improvements and innovations involve research and development, and the related work outputs are improved products, services, and systems. While some productivity gains can be made by improving work behaviors and work activities, the enormous gains in productivity over the last two decades have come from new and better work systems, particularly information systems. Information that was previously distributed by one person or one document can now be distributed throughout the world instantaneously via the Internet.

Ironically, as these systems do a better job of sharing information, demands and expectations for additional information often increase the workload instead of decrease it. Demands have been placed on computer experts since the beginning of this information revolution, and back-logs have required more scrutiny in tracking and prioritizing workload, budgeting, and outsourcing of work. Overall, we are seeing dramatic gains in work production and quality of life because of the information revolution.

By differentiating work inputs, processes, and outputs, the WPF provides some early indications as to why traditional examinations used to evaluate competencies are insufficient to account for the wide variation in work performance, and why a complete explanation of work performance goes well beyond any quick answer.

Outcomes and Impacts

In general systems theory, the outcomes and impacts of organizations are described as external results in the environment. Positive outcomes might include customer satisfaction or increased product sales, while impacts might be explained as the relative growth of the organization when compared to similar organizations. Outcomes and impacts of public programs might include the number or percentage of clients who entered the job market after completing a training program, and the resulting change in the unemployment rate.

Outcomes and impacts in the WPF are somewhat different from conventional thinking. Outcomes for a person within an organization include rewards (or punishments) that the worker receives from doing the work (or not doing it), and the impacts are the emotional, psychological, spiritual, and intellectual effects that these outcomes have on the worker. Thus psychology is very important to the study of HR management and work performance. Figure 1-3 provides an overview of these outcomes and impacts.

FIGURE 1-3 Work Performance Framework—Outcomes and Impacts

Outcomes	Impacts
Program Outcomes	Emotional
Program Benefits	Feelings
Unintended Consequences	
	Psychological
Human Resource Outcomes	Attitudes
Rewards	Judgments
Punishments	
Obligations	Intellectual
Adversities	Reasons
	Beliefs
Evaluation Outcomes	
Performance Measurements	Spiritual
Assessments of Fairness	Well-being

Outcomes

The WPF presents four sets of outcomes: program benefits and unintended consequences, rewards and punishments, obligations and adversities, and performance measurement and fairness. Unless an organization has a fair and accurate method for assessing performance, rewards and punishments will be subject to criticism. Thus, the need for civil service examinations to assess actual work performance, rather than just testing people for competencies, is perhaps the most revealing insight into effective public-sector HR management from the entire WPF.

Rewards are given for job successes and can be either intrinsic or extrinsic. Intrinsic rewards include job satisfaction, i.e., enjoying the work itself, and a pleasant work environment, which might include friendly people and comfortable surroundings. Extrinsic rewards include salary and benefits, promotions, special assignments, work opportunities, and the prestige or status that comes with the position.

Punishments are meted out for failures due to incompetence and for violations due to misconduct. Penalties can also be either intrinsic or extrinsic by reducing job satisfaction, salary, benefits, opportunities, or work status. Unfortunately, punishments are often in the eye of the beholder, so when a worker is not rewarded according to her expectations, she may view the outcome as a punishment. This phenomenon is especially visible where there are few promotions to hand out, and it often results in a person's transferring to another assignment or leaving the organization altogether.

Obligations are inherent work responsibilities; they are different from expectations, where judgments are made about how well that person is expected to perform in the context of the assignment. Obligations can accompany both rewards and punishments. For rewards, a new promotion may mean that you are obliged to take on additional work or more responsibility. People who expect their work to be easier following a promotion are usually deluding themselves. Obligations related to punishments are those corrections necessary to ensure satisfactory performance, and they may be required as a condition of retention.

Adversities are also likely to accompany promotions and special assignments. The adversity of danger exists in such fields as law enforcement and fire protection, but there are also many less obvious adversities. There are personality conflicts and challenges to authority; there are time constraints from longer days, more deadlines, and a heavier workload that require time-management skills; and there are greater risks from greater responsibilities and potential failures that require risk-management skills. These adversities require mental and physical strength to resist criticisms and attacks. Often, these adversities lead people to believe that they may not be up to the job, so they decline the promotion or special assignment.

Performance measurement is presented as an outcome in the WPF because employers must evaluate how well a program met the organization's goals, who should be rewarded or punished, and who can be expected to take on additional obligations and adversities.

When eligible lists are used for promotions and appointments in the public service, it is essential that the results are valid, i.e., the top performers appear at the top of the eligible list and vice versa. When eligible lists have low validity and utility, a no-win situation occurs, where managers look for alternative ways to reward the high performers and avoid promoting the low performers. Such actions often lead unions and disgruntled workers to make accusations of special treatment and unfairness. Problems are compounded by pressure for political favoritism to reward members of the political team that won office, further undercutting the credibility of the program managers.

Fair treatment has four components: equity, equality, due process and right to dissent, and the social contract. Equity requires that individuals receive special rewards based on special performance. Equality means that all workers are entitled to good benefits and respect. The right to dissent and due process procedures entitle the worker to present objections to the way she is treated based on claims of inequity—e.g., not receiving special rewards for special work—or inequality—e.g., not being well-treated as a member of the organization. Claims of unfair treatment are generally carried out according to union contracts, and unions may provide legal and technical services to their members to support their cases. Finally, the worker is expected to abide by the social contract—that is, because she has been given the benefits of equity, equality, the right to dissent, and due process, she is expected to be a good citizen of the organization.

Two other concepts go beyond the normal boundaries of fairness—generosity and mercy. Generosity requires us to help the needy and assist the underprivileged, not because they have earned the right for benevolent assistance but because of our humanitarian concerns.

Mercy is redemption; it affords a person a second chance. Some people make blunders that will forever prevent them from recovering under a system of strict merit and fair treatment. Only mercy offers the prospect of someone turning his or her life around and returning to the arms of society as an equal. Without the merciful act of a second chance, he or she may feel forever doomed. Even generosity and mercy have their limits, but the exceptional organization is the one that not only believes in fair treatment but also understands and practices generosity and mercy.

Impacts

Impacts are the emotional, psychological, intellectual, and spiritual effects that work outcomes have on the employee. It takes a great deal of fair and reliable treatment for an organization to gain the trust and affiliation of its workers, an exchange that works both ways. It takes a great deal of productive work and allegiance on the part of the worker to gain the trust and affiliation of the organization's leaders.

Three impacts in the WPF are emotional, intellectual, and psychological reactions to work; they roughly parallel Freud's mental structure of the id, the ego, and the superego. The fourth impact is the spiritual reaction that addresses the worker's overall well-being. In the WPF the dominant impact is intellectual because the intellect takes into consideration our emotions, our judgments, and our well-being in order to develop beliefs about the world we live in. We then apply these beliefs when making life decisions.

APPLYING THE WORK PERFORMANCE FRAMEWORK TO WORKFORCE PLANNING

The following overview of workforce planning shows how the WPF can be used as a tool for setting strategic HR goals.

Workforce planning has presented challenges for HR professionals ever since we realized that the baby boom generation would someday retire and test society's ability to replace them in the workforce and provide for their benefits in retirement. To heighten the impact of the baby boomers' retirement, people are living longer, and providing health care will present a major fiscal problem. Older workers must recognize that in 15 years or less, the value of fixed retirement income can be cut in half, so living longer will often translate to working longer. Retirees will need to decide how they can serve as active partners in the workforce, whether by volunteering or by working part-time. Public-sector organizations need to plan for increased services for older Americans, find a succeeding generation of workers, and use the talents of older workers to fill the HR gap.

In the past, workforce planning consisted largely of finding administrative support workers to process paper transactions—e.g., filing documents and other clerical work. Positions were classified en masse under a firm, consistent hierarchy, and tests for evaluating general mental ability were used to fill a broad range of government positions. Today, workforce planning is competency-driven: while general mental abilities have retained a credible role in employment test literature, organizations concentrate on recruiting people with specialized skills and abilities and use internal and external training programs to fine-tune those competencies.

Business records are now predominantly computerized, so filing documents and other clerical work have decreased or become unnecessary, and fewer support staff are needed. According to the New York State Department of Civil Service's *New York State Workforce Management Report 2006*, the number of employees in the state workforce decreased from 178,757 in 1996 to 164,314 in 2006, a decline of 8.1 percent. The number of administrative support workers decreased by more than 25 percent during that period, from 36,804 to 27,489, accounting for nearly 2 out of every 3 jobs lost over that decade.

Clearly, planning for the future workforce is extremely important, but relying on past trends may not provide an accurate picture of future HR needs. HR managers must have a clear picture of what their organization wants to achieve in the future, and what human resources will be needed to reach their goals.

Desirable Human Resource Outcomes

To conduct workforce planning, the HR department must clearly define the outcomes it seeks. As a starting point for discussion, the U.S. Office of Personnel Management (OPM) lists four categories for measuring the performance of HR programs in the federal government, along with descriptions of the categories and examples:

- Human Resources Operational Efficiency
- Measures of Legal Compliance
- Human Resource Management Program Effectiveness
- Strategic Alignment.

Operational Efficiency

An example of operational efficiency is the cost per discrete HR service—e.g., how much it costs, on average, to fill one position or train one person—or aggregated services—e.g., how much it costs to provide staffing services for all agency programs or train all agency personnel in one year. Total HR program costs as a ratio of all organizational costs is an efficiency measure that can be compared to similar organizations to determine whether total HR costs are higher or lower than they should be.

Another measure of efficiency is HR service processing time, or "cycle time." For example, one measure of efficiency is the "position fill cycle time," or the average amount of time it takes to fill a position from the time a request is made. By looking at service times, an analyst can identify which activities involve the greatest amount of staff time and which activities take the longest or shortest time to complete. For example, one might find that 80 percent of all recruitment and selection activities involve just 20 percent of all job openings. Thus, special attention can be given to reduce position fill cycle times for this 20 percent of job openings to maximize the cost-benefit return on HR processes.

Legal Compliance

Legal compliance involves meeting the requirements of all laws entitling workers, job applicants, or constituents to certain procedures or benefits. In the public sector, personnel actions such as appointments, transfers, leaves, and separations are processed in accordance with merit-system principles that involve specific requirements and supporting documentation.

Many of the complaints about "red tape" involve the documentation required to complete a personnel action. For example, after an appointment to a particular position is made, an HR staffer might have to document why another eligible candidate was not selected for the position. Explanations might include failure to respond to a canvass letter, declination based on job location, or temporary unavailability. Even though these requirements add time and cost to completing the appointment process, they guard against abuses and cronyism.

Program Effectiveness

HR program effectiveness relates to the benefits and unintended outcomes of these programs. Do the HR programs meet the needs of the organization and its program managers? Are program managers filling the positions that need to be filled? Are the workers getting the training they need?

Strategic Alignment

Strategic alignment means that the strategies and operations of the HR programs are aligned with the strategies of the organization, so the organization is able to meet its objectives, in part because the HR manager has set objectives and achieved performance goals that strengthen the organization.

Human Resource Service Objectives

HR service objectives can be constructed by comparing the OPM categories for performance measurement with the seven parts of the WPF. These objectives can be summarized as follows:

1. HR managers meet organizational *staffing needs* through position classification, recruitment, examination, selection, retention, and layoff programs.

2. HR managers meet *employee development needs* for the organization through traineeship, training, and development programs.

3. HR managers meet organizational *performance management needs* through programs for time and attendance, performance management, probation evaluation, performance evaluation, labor relations, and HR information systems.

4. HR managers meet organizational *diversity, fairness, and legal compliance needs* through the organization's affirmative action program and by completing personnel transactions according to legal and procedural requirements.

5. HR managers meet *employee benefits and rewards needs* for the organization through its promotion examinations, payroll services, employee benefits, workers' compensation, and employee recognition programs.

6. HR managers meet *work environment needs* of a healthy, positive, friendly, and respectful work environment through organizational and employee health and well-being programs and through employee assistance program.

These six HR service objectives can be used to evaluate the efficiency and effectiveness of specific HR programs, and to develop three HR strategic objectives: building HR capacity, building HR performance, and building HR community.

Building HR capacity is accomplished through the first two HR service objectives of staffing and employee development and relates to the first two parts of the WPF—human resources and enablers, the subjects of Chapters 2 and 3, respectively.

Building HR performance is accomplished through the third HR service objective pertaining to performance management and relates predominantly to the middle three parts of the WPF—inputs, processes, and outputs, the subjects of Chapters 4, 5, and 6, respectively.

Building HR community is accomplished through the last three HR service objectives that pertain to diversity, fairness, legal compliance, employee rewards and benefits, and the work environment. These topics relate to the last two parts of the WPF—outcomes and impacts, the subjects of Chapters 7 and 8, respectively.

The WPF makes the necessary connection between organizational goals and the human resources within the organization. The following chapters explain how the HR manager can use the WPF to align HR strategic objectives, HR service objectives, and HR programs to develop measurements for evaluating program efficiency and effectiveness. These insights should prove highly valuable for meeting the HR challenges of the 21st century.

The Human Resource

This chapter presents an overview of staffing the organization—creating the right positions, hiring people with the necessary abilities to fill those positions, and taking into consideration the socioeconomic conditions of people seeking employment. The chapter applies the Work Performance Framework (WPF) to staffing activities and reviews selected research findings on the general mental abilities and personality traits that affect staffing the organization. It then discusses specific human resource (HR) staffing programs used to (1) create positions; (2) recruit new workers and increase diversity; (3) promote, deploy, and redeploy existing workers; and (4) reduce staff levels when necessary. Finally, the chapter identifies several key measures for building human capital within an organization and discusses some implications for future staffing activities that warrant further research.

HUMAN RESOURCES IN THE WORK PERFORMANCE FRAMEWORK

The WPF describes three aspects of people as a human resource—their mental abilities, their physical abilities, and their socioeconomic background. (See Figure 2-1, "Work Performance Framework—Human Resources.")

FIGURE 2-1 Work Performance Framework—Human Resources

Mental Ability General Mental Ability Personality
Physical Ability Fitness Health
Socioeconomic Conditions Social Financial

Merit-system principles require that appointments and promotions be based on the applicant's qualifications for a position, where practicable, through competitive examinations. While the greatest attention is placed on mental abilities and some attention is placed on physical abilities, one of the roles of government is to help people who are disadvantaged by disabilities or unfavorable socioeconomic backgrounds. These requirements, which seem to conflict with one another, must be reconciled when filling positions in the public sector.

Mental Abilities

Figure 2-1 presents mental abilities as potential abilities, as opposed to inputs, which are applied abilities. Upon joining an organization, a person might need to learn operational requirements or refine his mental abilities to meet specialized organizational performance requirements. When recruiting new staff, an organization must decide whether it needs people with specialized knowledge, skills, and abilities (KSAs) to do the work or people with general mental abilities who can be trained to acquire the KSAs once hired. Often, dual strategies are employed to allow people with a specialized background to be appointed to a journey-level position, while generalists enter into a traineeship.

Figure 2-1 presents two categories of mental abilities—general mental ability and personality. While intelligence has been described in many ways, including attributes such as aptitude, wisdom, charisma, talent, and creativity, the WPF uses the term *general mental ability* or *g*, to describe the mental abilities that can be developed into KSAs required to perform specific work. The term *intelligence*, on the other hand, is presented in Chapter 8 as the beliefs and understanding we form as we experience and learn from all of life's events.

Personality traits, which the WPF identifies as the second set of mental abilities, were out of fashion for many years in evaluating merit and qualification for a position. Personality evaluations were considered vulnerable to subjective biases by raters and unreliable because they could be faked.

With the growth in customer service requirements, however, personality has resurfaced as a factor of job performance and in the screening process of job applicants. In courts over the last two decades, plaintiffs alleging discriminatory hiring practices have been required to demonstrate not only adverse impact but also discriminatory intent by the defendant. This has facilitated public sector organizations in evaluating personality traits during the screening process.

The most popular model in the literature of personality traits is the "big five"—extraversion, emotional stability, conscientiousness, agreeableness, and openness to experience (Funder 2001). Integrity tests, which are a type of personality test, have become popular screening devices used to reduce the probability of counterproductive job behaviors such as drinking, using drugs, fighting, stealing, or sabotaging equipment or operations.

Many aspects of general mental abilities and personality attributes must be considered when recruiting new people to an organization. Often there are trade-offs that must be acknowledged because each job requires an analysis of its important duties, the organizational environment, the work structure, and the competencies to perform the work. General mental ability and personality are HR abilities that potentially can be improved to some degree by training and development to perform specific work. Both are addressed in more detail in this chapter's selected literature review.

Physical Abilities

Unusual physical abilities and agility are usually needed only in protective service positions requiring physical exertion, such as police officers and firefighters, or in positions that may require heavy lifting. Because of innate physical differences between men and women, including differences in strength, requirements for the protective services involving physical ability, physical agility, and height/weight standards have come under a great deal of scrutiny over the past few decades. As a result, performance standards on physical agility tests have in many cases been either eliminated or adjusted by setting separate standards for men and women. These changes have allowed more women to enter the ranks of the protective services.

Physical ability includes the factor of effort in work performance. High performers have not only the mental capacity and personality to deal with complex work situations, but also the energy and stamina to remain effective under the adverse conditions of long workdays, strained relationships, in-fighting, tight deadlines, and failing ventures. Energy level is not typically viewed as an attribute of physical fitness, nor is it heavily emphasized in professional literature as a necessity for public-sector jobs or in job analysis. However, energy level often appears in advertisements for private-sector jobs. In the public sector, physical abilities and physical agility tests are generally narrowly construed as a minimum requirement or overlooked entirely, instead of seen as a factor that can predict high performance.

Title I of the *Americans with Disabilities Act of 1990* prohibits private employers, state and local governments, employment agencies, and labor unions from discriminating against qualified individuals with disabilities in job application procedures, hiring, firing, advancement, compensation, job training, and other terms, conditions, and privileges of employment (EEOC 2008). While there is a legitimate interest in hiring energetic people, employers must not assume that a person with a disability has a low energy threshold or work limitations. The tendency among HR managers in the public sector has been to err on the side of including employees with disabilities rather than excluding them.

Jobs are often set aside specifically to be filled by the disabled. Section 55-b of New York State's Civil Service Law authorizes the state government to fill up to 1,200 positions of the total workforce with people who are certified as disabled. Section 55-c authorizes the state to fill up to 300 additional positions with veterans who have a disability. These 1,500 positions are in the noncompetitive class, which means that a disabled applicant must meet the prescribed minimum qualifications for the position but is not required to compete for the position by taking a civil service examination.

People with mental health disabilities generally enjoy the same protections as those with physical disabilities, but mental disability may be more difficult to quantify and isolate, as it often varies in its manifestation from one day to the next. Mental health problems can be due to medical conditions, working conditions, or environmental conditions, such as stressors from family problems, financial problems, or transportation difficulties.

Drug or alcohol dependency might surface as a symptom of a mental health problem, and it can eventually become a problem in itself. Often, when a person is under a treatment program, he is protected from disciplinary action for his addiction but still subject to discipline for failing to meet performance standards. A person might be granted a leave of absence due to a disability, but after a fixed period of time, he or she can be terminated if still unable to return to work and perform at a minimum standard.

Socioeconomic Background

A person's socioeconomic background can have a strong influence on how she performs in a position. Some groups, such as African Americans, have long experienced discrimination in housing and employment. People living at the poverty level endure many financial hardships. The public sector has an obligation to address injustices, and employment laws and practices reflect these concerns.

A stream of federal and state legislation, beginning with the national Civil Rights Act of 1964, has made it illegal to discriminate based on group differences such as gender, race, age, ethnicity, sexual orientation, religion, or national origin, with particular attention given to equal access to housing and employment.

Veterans, as a specially designated group, receive extra points on civil service examinations and in some cases, absolute preference where their names are placed at the very top of an eligible list. Disabled veterans receive further preference within the group of veterans. Veterans are also often afforded preferred retention rights during layoffs. These benefits are viewed as partial payment for their special service to the country during times of war and other military conflicts.

In general, American society is wealthier today than at any other time in its history. Still, economic inequality is quite striking, with the wealthy able to live in very expensive homes and send their children to private schools and colleges, while the majority of people live in the middle class and strive to pay bills on time, send their children to college, and save for retirement. While their day-to-day needs may be taken care of, members of the middle class often have substantial debt and fall behind in saving for a rainy day or retirement.

People living in poverty have even harsher difficulties to face in paying for transportation, childcare, health care, and housing, which exacerbate their general financial difficulties. Children who live under difficult socioeconomic circumstances may face problems in early childhood development and self-esteem. Their deprivation may lead to acting out, promiscuity, and violence, which undermine their chances of getting a good education and finding a good job.

Affirmative action programs, set-asides for disabled workers, and other programs to benefit minority populations and disadvantaged people are important issues for public-sector recruitment and selection programs. They are addressed in Chapter 7 from the theoretical perspective of fairness.

SELECTED LITERATURE REVIEW

The literature review for this chapter addresses two key factors under the mental ability portion of the WPF—general mental ability and personality, which are prominent areas of concern to HR managers when staffing their organizations. General mental abilities were a cornerstone of standardized testing for much of the 20th century, and a strong interest in personality traits has resurfaced over the last decade due to a renewed emphasis on work habits, personality conflicts, and difficulties in working well with other people in a team environment. General mental abilities and personality attributes are transformed into competencies, or job-related KSAs, through training and development.

General Mental Ability

General mental ability or *g* is presented as a key component in the first part of the WPF. This section includes some history on tests for general mental ability and discusses other concepts related to mental abilities such as intelligence.

How valid is general mental ability? Validity figures explain the correlation between test scores and work performance, which can then be used to evaluate the usefulness of the test in screening for the best candidates.

However, because of imperfect testing methods and population samples, various studies report statistical and measurement errors related to validity figures. Using meta-analyses of validity studies, researchers have been able to correct for these effects (Schmidt and Hunter 1998; Hunter and Schmidt 1990; Hunter et al. 1982). In their extensive research on various selection methods over the past 85 years, including employment tests, interviews, reference checks, and education, Schmidt and Hunter (1998) report that the maximum corrected validity in their study tops out at .65 using test scores for general mental ability in combination with integrity tests, which assess certain personality traits. They conclude that general mental ability (*g*) is the best predictor of job performance, particularly when used in conjunction with integrity tests.

Sternberg and Kaufman (1998) discuss intelligence as an attribute of human abilities from the perspectives of culture, psychometrics, and theories on intelligence. They note that general Western psychological views of intelligence include three components—the ability to learn, the ability to adapt to the environment, and the ability to understand and control oneself (metacognition). Depending on the culture of the people being studied, other civilizations' views on intelligence include topics in mental processing, benevolence, integrity, humility, interpersonal intelligence or social competence, memory, problem solving, technological skills, creative thinking, and even silence.

Sternberg and Kaufman assert that the history of psychometrics began with tests of general mental ability, or *g*, but are now evolving toward more dynamic or interactive testing. But they note that these newer tests have not been thoroughly validated and are more promissory than proven. Among the theories they discuss, three are of particular interest—emotional intelligence, Howard Gardner's theory of multiple intelligences, and the theory of successful intelligence advanced by Sternberg.

Emotional intelligence includes the abilities to perceive, appraise, and express emotions, generate relevant feelings, understand emotions, and promote growth (Sternberg and Kaufman 1998; Mayer and Salovey 1997). Dulewicz and Higgs (2004) identify self-awareness, emotional resilience, motivation, interpersonal sensibility, intuitiveness, and conscientiousness as elements of emotional intelligence.

Sternberg and Kaufman note that Gardner's theory of multiple intelligences includes linguistic, logical-mathematical, spatial, musical, bodily-kinesthetic, interpersonal, and intrapersonal intelligences as separate human intelligences that are based in part on separate brain operations. Gardner has more recently proposed the possibility of an additional intelligence—naturalist intelligence, which is an ability to understand nature and living things.

Practical intelligence includes analytical, creative, and practical abilities. Analytical abilities are used to develop strategies for personal success based on an analysis of one's strengths and weaknesses. Creative abilities are attributed to identifying undervalued ideas and exploiting them. The practical abilities, or practical intelligence, advanced by Sternberg involves "the acquisition and use of tacit knowledge, which is knowledge of what one needs to know to succeed in a given environment that is not explicitly taught and that usually is not verbalized" (494).

Two weaknesses of these evolving theories of intelligence are the inability to develop reliable standardized tests that are affordable and, when tests are developed, the inability to guard against a candidates' ability to "study for the test" or learn how to do well on the test as an end in itself.

Thus, we return to general mental ability (*g*) as the mental ability best evaluated and most useful for predicting work performance. However, this does not mean general mental ability explains all work performance. Despite these findings, Murphy et al. (2003) reported that the respondents in a survey of 703 members of the Society for Industrial and Organizational Psychologists had some misgivings about tests for general mental ability. Their respondents believed that although these tests are fair and valid, they provide incomplete measures of intelligence and the different abilities or attributes that affect performance. The respondents also wanted to avoid any adverse impacts these tests have on employment opportunities for minorities.

Thus, while a solid review of test validity over the last 85 years concludes that tests for general mental ability are the most valid form of testing when used in conjunction with integrity tests, researchers continue to look for other methods of evaluating and selecting candidates for employment. This leads us to the second component of mental ability in the WPF—personality.

Personality

Funder (2001) notes that in personality psychology—the branch of psychology that links personality with behavior—personality traits, behaviorism, and social-cognition are three of the most prominent contemporary personality paradigms. According to Funder, personality traits have been well defined by empirical research, and he cites the "big five" personality traits of extraversion, neuroticism (sometimes evaluated as emotional stability), conscientiousness, agreeableness, and openness to experience as dominant in the literature.

Mount and Barrick (1995) provide an extensive analysis of the big five and show how these personality traits have been evaluated in numerous studies. Although none of the studies they reference match these five attributes exactly, the comparisons are obvious when presented as a group.

For example, terms describing forms of *extraversion* include power, surgency, social extraversion, social, talkativeness, and expressiveness. Terms describing forms of *agreeableness* include warm, friendly, cooperative, and courteous. Terms describing forms of *conscientiousness* include responsible, orderly, hard-working, thorough, and dependable. Terms describing forms of *neuroticism* include anxiety, emotional instability, depression, guilt, emotional, self-protective, and excitable. And finally, terms describing forms of *openness to experience* include intelligent, curious, cultured, and broad-minded.

Behaviorism, as Funder explains, began with the ambition of its founders, John Watson and B.F. Skinner, "to excise from psychology all that is subjective and unobservable" (201). Their research led to studying how the environment and imposed reinforcements affected observable behavior. Funder further notes that, more recently, social-learning theorists point out that often the *beliefs* about potential reinforcements direct behaviors rather than the *actual reinforcements*, which has led to further research on how we develop our beliefs about the world we live in and how people with different beliefs may behave differently.

Social cognition theory primarily focuses on how the individual understands himself and behaves in ways that are consistent with that self-perception and goals. Thus the underlying concept of social cognition is for a person to understand himself and act knowledgeably. Funder (2001) discusses the work of Albert Bandura, who explains that a self-system can be developed "as the result of the interaction of the person and his or her environment, which allows self-control through self-reward and self-punishment—a basis for moral behavior" (204). The implication here is that when a person knows himself and understands his environment, he is able to maximize the use of certain behaviors to serve his self-interests.

In addition to cognitive understanding of the self, Mischel and Shoda (1998) integrate knowing and understanding one's feelings or affective state into an expanded theory of a "cognitive-affective personality system" or CAPS. Thus, self-control and self-determination are not only a cognitive act, but also one that derives the most meaning emotionally.

In the WPF, personality traits, like general mental abilities, are presented as a human resource. Self-efficacy and expectancy theory, which are aspects of social cognition theory, are linked to effort, energy, and intentions as work inputs in Chapter 4. Behavioral aspects of personality are presented as work behaviors in the WPF and discussed in Chapter 5. Work behaviors are determined by our work inputs, by the constraints dictated to us by work rules, and by the consequent rewards or punishments we receive.

Intelligence, including emotional intelligence, is presented in the WPF as an impact that affects our beliefs and understanding of the world. Unlike Gardner (Sternberg and Kaufman 1998), the WPF proposes that intelligence is not just innate, but rather a combination of both innate abilities and learned beliefs. This difference is discussed in Chapter 8.

While individuals are constrained by their personality traits, just as they are by their mental abilities, people also have a considerable capacity to overcome areas of weakness through education, training, and experience. The WPF envisions a greater capacity to adjust behaviors irrespective of personality traits than is perhaps suggested by the psychological literature on personality. Moreover, in the modern workplace, high expectations are placed on a worker to be a part of a team environment, so information on appropriate work behaviors is more readily available than in the past. Adhering to organizationally prescribed work behaviors is very important to successful work performance.

Thus, we present general mental ability (g) and personality as the core mental abilities in the WPF. While we acknowledge the existence of other mental abilities, traits like emotional intelligence can be accounted for at the resource stage as a combination of general mental ability and personality. Moreover, we suggest that intelligence is not a resource, but an intellectual reaction to our life experiences. We will discuss intelligence further at the impact stage of the WPF in Chapter 8.

Mount and Barrick (1995), in discussing personality traits and related HR management issues, note that "[o]ne of the most pressing research needs in human resources management is the development of a comprehensive theory of work performance" (154). The WPF provides the structure for a comprehensive theory of work performance and incorporates personality traits, social cognition theory, and behaviors into its many components.

STAFFING PROGRAMS

Staffing programs are designed to bring human resources (people) into the organization to perform work and produce outputs. HR managers meet their staffing goals through a number of staffing programs, including position classification, examinations, recruitment, selection, retention, and layoffs. Position classification, which involves work processes, duties, and activities, is discussed in Chapter 5. This section presents a brief discussion of each of the other staffing programs.

Examinations

A variety of examinations are used to fill positions in the public sector, including written tests, training and experience examinations, oral tests, assessment centers, and performance assessments. After these examinations, eligible lists are created to certify interested and eligible candidates. Examinations evaluate whether a candidate possesses the critical competencies or KSAs to perform the necessary work. Job interviews, although used in the selection process, do not determine the final score or rank on an eligible list and so are not presented as an examination. Job interviews are discussed later in the chapter under recruitment and selection.

Written Tests

Written tests are the most common type of examination because large candidate pools can be tested quickly and there is a sense of fair play because the scores cannot be manipulated. Test validity generally runs in the range of .35–.40 for written tests. Test validity is a correlation coefficient that measures the correlation between candidate test scores and job performance. It can range from 1.0 to -1.0, with 1.0 indicating a perfect correlation between test scores and job performance and -1.0 indicating a perfect negative correlation, which would mean the worst candidates appear at the top of the eligible list and the best candidates at the bottom. A test with a validity coefficient of 0.0 means there is no correlation between test scores and job performance; these results equate to random chance.

Written examinations can evaluate general mental abilities through questions that test attributes such as verbal abilities, numeric abilities, or spatial relations, or they can test for precise KSAs related to specific jobs and job categories. While the findings of Schmidt and Hunter (1998) show that tests of general mental abilities generate the highest validity coefficients, legal defenses of test plans rely heavily on job analysis that links test questions to specific competencies or KSAs, in accordance with guidelines issued by the Equal Employment Opportunity Commission.

For most promotion examinations, workers have had the opportunity to gain job-related KSAs such as knowledge of agency rules, regulations, and operational procedures. Since they need to know this information to perform the work, questions on agency operations and procedures are directly job-related. For candidates recruited from outside the organization, job-related KSAs might include knowledge of a technical field such as computer programming.

Training and Experience Examinations

Examinations that evaluate a candidate's past training and experience are used for hard-to-fill positions, often where the candidate search is noncompetitive and the ability to make a swift job offer is critical for getting the best person. Written examinations often take several months to complete, involving test development, administration, and grading, whereas training and experience examinations can be administered at once.

Training and experience examinations are often used for certain professional positions that require special licenses or certifications, since candidates have already been required to pass a professional examination. Candidates are required to complete a form that asks a series of questions related to their educational accomplishments and experiences. Test administrators might give credit for grade-point average, higher educational degrees, degrees most appropriate to the job, special credentials, and job-related experience.

While some studies of training and experience examinations have generated very low test-validity coefficients, the low validity is usually offset by larger bands of candidates on the eligible list or small pools of candidates where any candidate who applies is eligible for selection.

Oral Tests

Oral tests have been very popular but are rather expensive to hold, with the cost per candidate far exceeding the cost for a written test when there is a large candidate field. When the candidate field is very small, however, oral tests can actually be less expensive. At the New York State Department of Civil Service, the three factors most frequently evaluated during an oral test are a candidate's ability to (1) reason clearly and make sound judgments, (2) communicate effectively, and (3) establish effective work relationships.

Besides cost, a drawback of oral tests (as opposed to written tests) is the appearance that they are subjective. Criticisms are often based on inter-rater variation in rater severity and within-rater variation of rater severity (Wilson and Wang, 1995). Some raters are harder, some are easier, and the same rater may be harder or easier on different candidates.

Criticisms are also based on "halo" errors, which according to Fisicaro and Lance (1990) can take three forms: the general-impression model, the salient dimension model, and the inadequate discrimination model. The general-impression model occurs as a halo error when a general impression affects scores of several or all of the test dimensions. The salient dimension model occurs when the rater's score for one dimension influences the scores on other dimensions. The inadequate discrimination model occurs when the rater fails to identify which candidate behaviors are assigned to the various dimensions. Like written tests, validity coefficients for oral tests generally range between .35 and .40.

Assessment Centers

Assessment centers evaluate a variety of factors and are often used to recruit people for top-level positions. Assessment centers may ask candidates to complete an oral test, an interview, and other group interactions or exercises that demonstrate leadership and command. They might also include a battery of technical tests that measure various competencies.

While quite expensive to administer, assessment centers are used when the consequences of making a poor choice can place an organization at substantial risk. Still, an assessment center is likely to produce a validity coefficient comparable to that of oral tests and written tests, raising questions about its cost-effectiveness.

Performance Assessments

Performance assessments examine a promotion candidate's job performance over the previous several years. This author has used performance assessments in conjunction with other tests and achieved test validity coefficients approaching .90, far exceeding any other form of examination.

The reason for the high validity is that the job performance scores used to evaluate test validity are also part of the examination. Performance assessments can be very time-consuming and expensive to administer, and they can be used for promotion candidates only when claims about past job performance can be verified. (Performance assessments are discussed in more detail in Chapter 7.)

Eligible Lists

Once the examinations have been completed, eligible lists are created and maintained to certify to program managers the names of candidates who are interested and eligible for appointment. The results of the responses from candidates who are canvassed from the eligible lists are recorded on the lists, such as "interested" in the appointment or "temporarily unavailable." Once an operating division has made a selection, information on appointments and declinations is posted to the eligible lists.

Overall, the low test validity of most examinations raises questions about the usefulness of the eligible lists compiled from the tests. As a result, even when there are sufficient candidates, agencies may seek flexibility in selecting a candidate, usually unsuccessfully.

The "rule of three," which is used in many states, requires that a candidate be selected from among the three highest-standing candidates on an eligible list. At times, agencies may be required to choose between selecting one of three entirely unsatisfactory candidates who happened to perform well on the test or leaving the position unfilled until another agency selects one of the three. This problem is especially likely to occur when a large number of appointments are being made, placing a greater strain on agencies that may need to fill multiple jobs.

To overcome this problem, some states have turned to "band" scoring by concluding that test scores within a certain range are comparable, and all candidates within the band are given the same consideration for appointment, thus enlarging the group from which a candidate may be hired. Still, problems remain for lists where agencies may have made so many appointments that the highest band or bands are still reduced to three unsatisfactory candidates.

An alternative recommendation is to have a "rule of ten," although this would expand the choice of candidates on very small lists to anyone who passed the test. Another option frequently discussed is to allow agencies to pass over a candidate who was deemed unacceptable at three separate job interviews. There is a risk in such proposals for increased appointment flexibility—the more flexibility there is, the greater chance of political favoritism, and the average person may not get the opportunity to compete on an equal footing with people who are well-connected.

Recruitment and Selection

Recruitment activities can involve many kinds of events, such as visits to colleges and universities or job fairs, community outreach programs to attract minority candidates, and paid advertisements. The Internet has become an important tool for recruiting candidates and for candidates to find employment opportunities.

Recruitment challenges are looming just ahead: the challenge to fill vacancies as large numbers of baby boomers retire over the next several years, and with a shortage of replacement workers. Some of the greatest concerns about worker shortages are in the field of health care, professional positions such as engineers and accountants, and high-level administrators. Part of the shortfall in health care providers is being dealt with through immigration. The Philippine Nurses Association of New York actively promotes the employment of Filipino nurses in New York (Philippine Nurses Association of New York, Inc., 2008)—an example not only of the increasing use of the Internet but also of how today's workforce is affected by globalization.

Recruitment challenges for public-sector agencies include getting a sufficient pool of highly qualified candidates and recruiting college students before they graduate and are hired by private companies. Some states address these challenges by using continuous recruitment examinations that evaluate training and experience. Candidates can apply at any time and receive their scores quickly instead of waiting several months for the results of a written test. Moreover, the scores are banded, so there are generally larger pools of candidates to consider.

Public agencies can recruit college students who are close to graduation but have not made other employment commitments, and often agencies will hire a college student as an intern as well. If the student shows promise and scores high enough on the examination, the agency will offer a permanent position upon graduation.

Another recruitment strategy is to allow agencies to offer salaries above the minimum entry level when the entry salary is not competitive in the job market. While government agencies are required to abide by the principle of equal pay for equal work, different regions may have higher housing and transportation costs. Geographic pay differentials can be available for areas with especially high costs of living.

While the selection process for public-sector agencies generally requires the use of eligible lists, a number of factors are considered at the interview. A candidate's oral presentation and interpersonal skills, general appearance, and level of interest in the position can have a strong influence on a decision to hire. Very often, the job interview offers a great opportunity to build HR capacity. A well-conducted interview can expose valuable strengths or significant concerns about a candidate.

Redeployment

Redeployment of a worker can occur by promotion, transfer, reassignment, or assignment to a special project. Promotion redeployment occurs when a person is promoted into another part of the organization or into a different job classification. Interdepartmental promotion eligible lists are used to promote a person to a different agency when that agency's departmental promotion list is exhausted.

To foster redeployment, promotion fields are sometimes broadened from direct-line titles to include collateral titles or a combination of salary grade and additional qualifications. For example, "You must be serving in a Grade 18 title or higher, and in addition, you must have had two years of experience in preparing or negotiating personnel service contracts or purchases for goods or equipment."

Transfers can be made to the same title in a different agency or to a different title in the same or different agency. In New York State government, transfers require the consent of both the agency and the individual. A reassignment is the movement of a worker from one position to another under the same title and appointing authority, and it does not require the consent of the worker. Often, however, a person will request a reassignment because of personality conflicts or workload problems.

An assignment to a special project can be a good opportunity to enhance one's resume. These short-term assignments generally involve several people from various parts of the organization brought together to address a particular problem or need. Many of these assignments involve computerization, where work previously completed by people is reconfigured to complete part of the work process electronically. Important connections can be made by getting to know other people in the organization and proving one's worth to them. However, unfavorable attributes can just as easily be exposed, which will thwart future opportunities for someone who is unhelpful or uninterested in the special assignment.

Equally important, new skills can be developed from these assignments, including project management skills, team skills, skills for building interpersonal relationships, and problem-solving skills. Volunteers for such assignments show initiative, particularly when they are required to simultaneously carry out their regular work duties. Organizations look closely at special project participants when planning for their future leaders.

Retention

Retention can be an effective tool for meeting staffing goals. Salaries, benefits, work environment, and job satisfaction generally contribute to a worker's decision to stay or leave. Employee satisfaction surveys, new employee surveys, and exit interviews and surveys can often identify reasons for employees' dissatisfaction or decisions to leave an organization, providing important information for improvements. The high retention rate of employees in the public sector suggests that job security, salaries, benefits, and quality of work life are quite attractive to many people. (Building HR community, which can be measured in part by retention and turnover rates, is discussed in Part 3.)

Layoffs

Layoffs in private industry often occur as a result of financial losses and downsizing, consolidation of functions, or computerization that eliminates the need for workers. In the public sector, where there is no invisible hand of the marketplace, layoffs appear to be more politically strategic. There may also be few political rewards for saving available money. While a new administration might come in and "clean house" because of financial problems created by a previous administration, there often seems to be a protocol of downsizing early in an administration, so funds are available later to build alliances and create new programs that will symbolize the achievements of the new administration. Ironically, when one administration is frugal and saves money, the next administration can benefit by choosing to spend the accumulated rainy day money.

Layoffs can often be avoided or minimized through normal attrition. In the 1990s, New York State adopted laws, rules, and policies to avoid layoffs by instead using redeployment lists and early retirement incentives. While "preferred lists" are used for people who have been demoted or laid off as a result of the abolition or reduction of positions, "redeployment lists" were created to redeploy people to vacated positions due to normal attrition rather than layoffs.

KEY PERFORMANCE MEASURES

The key question in measuring HR effectiveness is whether staffing programs are building the organization's capacity to meet current challenges and embrace future opportunities. The key performance questions for addressing efficiency are whether the program services are plentiful, timely, error-free, and provided at a reasonable cost. Since HR programs provide services, the unit of analysis is the transaction, which includes the service and the payment for the service. (Chapter 6 explores efficiency measures of services as outputs.)

Efficiency Measures

The primary staffing function lies in filling positions. Table 2-1 presents a hypothetical set of important measures for filling positions. The table is divided into four parts that relate to intake or position-fill requests, work production or the number of requests completed, backlog or number of requests not yet completed, and cycle time or the average time to fill a position in business days. Since internal fills are different from new hires, separate figures are presented for each, along with figures for all appointments.

TABLE 2-1 Sample Position Fill Measures			
	Positions Filled		
	All	**Promotions and Transfers**	**New Hires**
Intake – Requests to Fill Positions			
Annual Average 2004–2006	225	125	100
2007	250	125	125
Change	25	0	25
Production – # of Positions Filled			
Annual Average 2004–2006	224	128	96
2007	220	130	90
Change	–4	2	–6
Percent Change	–2%	2%	–6%
Target – Positions Filled	255	125	130
2007 vs. Target	–35	5	–40
Percent Over/Under Target	–14%	4%	–31%
Backlog – Requests Not Completed			
Start of 2007	125	50	75
End of 2007	155	45	110
Percent Change	24%	–10%	47%
Average Cycle Time, in Business Days			
Annual Average 2004–2006	47.0	35	63
2007	44.6	34	60
Change	–2.4	–1	–3
Percent Change	–5%	–3%	–5%
Target Cycle Times	45	35	55
2007 vs. Target	–0.4	–1.0	5.0

The first section on intake in Table 2-1 shows the annual average of new requests to fill a position for the three-year period of 2004–06, the number of requests for 2007, and the change. The annual average for 2004–06 is a baseline against which the 2007 results can be compared.

The second section, on production, shows the baseline yearly average of the number of positions filled during 2004–06, the figures for 2007, and the level of change. The table also provides production targets or production goals for 2007, along with comparisons of 2007 production levels against the target. As can be seen, the number of new hires for 2007 is well below the target. This suggests that either the target must be adjusted or a new initiative must be implemented to reach future goals.

The third section reports the backlog of fill requests and whether the backlog is increasing or decreasing. The backlog of requests for internal fills has decreased slightly, but increased dramatically for new hires. These figures provide further evidence for the need of a special initiative to address hiring new staff.

The fourth section of Table 2-1 shows how long it takes, on average, to fill a position. Since new hires must be recruited, it is to be expected that these appointments will take longer to fill than internal promotions. Still, due to the increased need to bring in new hires, the average time needs to be reduced. Thus the hiring initiative should concentrate not just on filling more positions but also on reducing the average cycle time.

Table 2-1 is a good example of applying key performance measures, but these measures do not tell the whole story. In fact, they raise more questions. How do we decrease our average position fill cycle time? Can we do it? Are there any negative consequences? The diamonds are in the details.

To present the kind of information shown in Table 2-1, data must be posted, processes tracked, and results calculated. In a real case, one agency processed approximately 2,500 appointments and promotions over a three-year period. The average fill time was 63 business days, including a finance review period, an administrative approval time, a review and approval period by the budget division, and recruitment and selection time. A closer look revealed that 23 titles—less than 10 percent of all titles filled during the three-year period—involved 65 percent of all agency appointments and 70 percent of all recruitment and selection time. It was obvious that reducing fill times for those critical titles would have the greatest impact on reducing average position fill cycle times.

These key performance measures for filling positions—intake, work production, backlog, and service cycle times—can be applied to all staffing activities. Although tracking performance does require data collection and analysis, spreadsheets maintained on desktop computers can often be used for the majority of these activities. A key point to remember is that the request for service begins the cycle time, and approval times affect the total service time.

Effectiveness Measures

Building HR capacity directly affects the capacity of an organization to complete its work and determines HR program effectiveness. As just noted, one indication of a more effective HR program is a decrease in the backlog of requests to fill positions. But how can we tell that organizational capacity is increasing and that HR programs are contributing to the improved state? Here are five ways:

- Measure the efficiency of HR programs

- Monitor organizational effectiveness from reports by the operating divisions on program performance

- Ask the operating divisions directly or with a survey

- Ask the employees directly or with a survey

- Ask your HR staff directly or with a survey.

The use of customer satisfaction surveys has increased dramatically in recent years because they serve as a feedback loop for vital information on the effectiveness of HR program services. But the use of surveys can be applied to all stakeholders—the executive staff, the program managers, the HR program managers, the employees, and the HR staff.

Organizational reports are a useful resource for determining whether the organization and its divisions are effective and where there might be weaknesses. Surveys of operating divisions and bureaus can also provide evidence about their own effectiveness, the effectiveness of HR services, and the relationship between the two. Feedback on HR staffing services might relate to staffing levels, the abilities of newly hired staff, or suggestions for new or revised recruitment or retention activities. Employee opinion surveys can disclose information about job satisfaction that can help improve HR retention programs and services.

Often, a well-constructed survey of HR staff can yield a formal list of improvement opportunities that might go unnoticed when offered in casual conversation. To eliminate mundane suggestions, preface the questions with a request for information that will significantly increase HR capacity, performance, and community, thus aligning improvement suggestions with strategic objectives. While there may be some value to minor improvements, too many suggestions can bog down the process, particularly when many have minimal expected benefits.

THE FUTURE STATE OF HUMAN RESOURCE MANAGEMENT AND RESEARCH OPPORTUNITIES

In the past, staffing activities did not have to be highly responsive to program managers' staffing needs because, once employed, people in government tended to stay in government. For example, as of January 2006 almost 65 percent of New York State employees had over 10 years of service with the state and over 34 percent had more than 20 years of service.

The major staffing concern in the state's 2006 *Workforce Report* is the rate at which baby boomers are becoming eligible for retirement. Over 36 percent of the people now employed by New York State will be 55 or older by 2010. At the federal level, the average age of retirement for the federal civilian workforce between 1995 and 2004 was 58, and the average years of service was 26.3 years. It is clear that baby boomer retirements will create a large number of vacancies, and there will be difficulty replacing people in the hard-to-fill positions.

Because of the trend toward mass computerization and continuous improvement in business processes, future staffing goals will likely need to be flexible in order to adjust to optimized work structures and staffing patterns. Both worker abundance and worker shortage require HR managers to anticipate the need to classify new positions or reclassify existing positions to ones requiring new skills and abilities, to carry out special recruitment initiatives, and to redeploy and retrain existing staff.

Because competing organizations are driving up the costs of high-value workers, HR managers are experiencing shortages in such areas as accounting, engineering, nursing, and general health care. There are also concerns about replacing the large number of top-level managers who are at or near retirement age.

Meanwhile, with the increasing costs of health care and retirement benefits, organizations are closely attuned to the marginal benefits of each new hire. This concern has given rise to the increased hiring of temporary and part-time workers for less essential services and the outsourcing of some functions to expert consultants. These employment arrangements allow the organization to provide few or no benefits and no tenure protection, so the services of these workers can be terminated at will.

HR managers will likely find that meeting future staffing goals will be quite a challenge. There will be a shortage of available workers in the coming years to replace the large number of baby boomers who have retired or are about to retire. Hopefully, able-bodied seniors will do their part to help fill the gaps where shortages might occur by extending their careers or returning to the workforce as consultants or on a part-time basis.

In the near future, three staffing situations are likely to develop. The first involves jobs where shortages will present some difficulties, but HR managers will be able to use strategies such as redeployment and retraining to address those shortages. The second situation involves highly specialized jobs that will be very difficult to fill and will require innovative ways to address shortages.

A third situation, which is already developing in the American workforce at large, is the growing number of unskilled or low-skilled workers who are relegated to minimum-wage jobs. Many of these workers have great difficulty finding better-paying jobs because they lack technical skills or because jobs are being outsourced to other countries.

Although solutions for these challenges may seem to go beyond the power of the individual public-sector HR manager, the academic community must research and address policy issues to help find solutions and identify the role of the public sector in helping low-skilled workers obtain useful, relevant training and experience that can lead to a better life.

When people are presented as a critical human resource to be recruited through a series of staffing programs and services, the various roles of the HR manager are magnified and clarified. Public-sector personnel managers must act strategically to meet staffing goals through a variety of programs. Those HR services involve job classification, recruitment, examinations, selection, retention, redeployment, and sometimes layoffs. Each HR program must be evaluated on its efficiency and its effectiveness in building HR capacity.

Critical concerns about shortages of qualified candidates are surfacing. Low-skilled workers are being replaced with computers and must look for different jobs because their present jobs may not exist in the future. Moreover, in a global society competition for jobs can be intense and can come from outside the United States. When competition is great, the unskilled worker finds a marketplace where jobs are at or near minimum wage levels. While HR managers in the public sector must continue to bring the best and brightest people into the organization, they must also be attuned to other social goals related to equal treatment and improving the lives of those who are disadvantaged.

Enablers: The Bridge to Success

I n the Work Performance Framework (WPF), the human resources described in Chapter 2—mental abilities, physical abilities, and socioeconomic conditions—become work inputs through the development process presented in this chapter. The key factors in the process are what the WPF terms *enablers*, which convert potential abilities to applied abilities.

This chapter presents a theoretical overview of employee training and development that goes beyond traditional thinking to include the process of fully enabling the worker and reveals the value of enablers and how to use them strategically. It begins with a discussion of enablers in the context of the WPF, enabling opportunities, and a selected literature review, and it follows with specific enabling programs and several key performance measures to evaluate their efficiency and effectiveness. The chapter concludes with a look into the future of employee-enabling activities and research opportunities.

BACKGROUND

Many organizations view employee training as no more than running an orientation for new employees and offering a small selection of training modules. In the WPF, however, the concept of employee development expands our understanding of employee training to include education, credentials, on-the-job training, and mentoring. By using the term enablers, the WPF broadens the conception of employee training and development even further.

Key to the enabling process is opportunity. Do workers have opportunities to grow and develop? Do they understand the value of various opportunities, and do they actively pursue them? Or do they instead accept just those opportunities clearly placed in front of them? Or, perhaps, do they actually thwart or reject opportunities that might dramatically improve their work performance, career success, and lives? All of us can identify instances where we benefited from some opportunities and missed out on others, but it is quite clear that the people who make the most of enabling opportunities are more likely to maximize their work performance and get the most out of life.

ENABLERS IN THE WORK PERFORMANCE FRAMEWORK

The WPF describes five categories of enablers—education and training, experience, associations, healthy living, and special programs. (See Figure 3-1, "Work Performance Framework—Enablers.")

FIGURE 3-1 Work Performance Framework—Enablers

Enablers	Benefits
Education and Training	*Learning* *Reasoning* *Simulating Experience*
Experience	*Empowerment* *Practice*
Associations	*Learning about* *Research and Trends* *Networking*
Healthy Living	*Good Health* *Vigor*
Special Programs	*Special Opportunities* *Aid*

Education and Training

Education and training are perhaps the first terms that come to mind when we think of preparing ourselves for the job market. Higher education teaches professional and technical competencies. At the community college level, a person might train to become a technical expert such as a plumber, automotive technician, electrician, or licensed practical nurse. Education at a community college can also serve as a stepping stone to a four-year school at a manageable cost, an important benefit for families with limited financial resources.

At the undergraduate and graduate levels, a person might obtain the education and competencies to become a lawyer, doctor, engineer, accountant, computer analyst, registered professional nurse, scientist, or teacher, to name just a few. Educational programs in public administration or business administration provide training for positions in management and administration. While education in a professional or technical field provides a direct link to the workplace, degrees in the liberal arts provide a broad view of the world in preparation for a more rounded life.

Organizational training programs often address competencies related to staff supervision and operational information on the pertinent laws, rules, regulations, policies, and procedures of the field. Special training programs include orientation for new employees, training on employment laws and legal and policy prohibitions against discrimination, and traineeship programs for inexperienced workers not yet ready for journey-level assignments, which require a full understanding of the particular work duties, work environment, and operational procedures. Training programs may also target competencies related to interpersonal relationships, oral presentation, special computer software, and customer service procedures and techniques.

Professional associations provide continuing educational courses to keep the professional worker abreast of trends and new findings in the field. Some continuing education programs are tied to professional examinations and advanced professional certifications. For example, the International Public Management Association for Human Resources (IPMA-HR) offers two certification programs for the public HR community: IPMA-Certified Professional (IPMA-CP) and IPMA-Certified Specialist (IPMA-CS).

Standard education provides the opportunity to learn various kinds of information, including the data and details relevant to a particular subject and the context for interpreting the information. At a higher level, education develops the ability to reason based on understanding underlying principles and theories, and it provides the skills to apply reason to new situations. Reasoning skills enable a person in the public service to solve problems, envision improvements and innovations, develop better policies and procedures, and pursue changes to existing laws, rules, and regulations.

Experience

Experience can be gained directly through appointments and promotions, or indirectly through special assignments, internships, or even volunteer work. This experience can be valuable in developing interpersonal skills and influencing techniques in a work environment, delegating work to others and monitoring their performance, and managing resources and workload. Becoming the leader of an activity is an important way to understand what a leader is seeking from her staff, and the earlier this information is learned, the better.

Leadership requires important traits like loyalty, commitment, reliability, and friendliness. These lessons are very important to the worker when she seeks someone to champion her cause for that next promotion or special assignment, and people who fail to learn these lessons may find themselves disenfranchised from important organizational leaders.

A vital part of on-the-job experience is guidance from a mentor or coach who can share valuable lessons and assist the new worker in understanding the culture and values of an organization, including actions that get rewarded and can increase the likelihood of success at work, as well as the taboos that will mark a person as someone to distrust or avoid.

Associations

Involvement in professional associations, community and alumnae organizations, and political parties provides opportunities to work with highly motivated and capable people who can share lessons about their experiences. Professional conferences can help people keep up on new trends in their fields. Making a presentation at a conference can help a person develop oral presentation skills, while submitting articles to professional journals for publication can help refine the skill of communicating ideas in writing. Finally, networks from these associations often open doors to new opportunities; building networks and nurturing relationships are key attributes for leading an organization.

Healthy Living

Organizations often promote healthy living by sponsoring such activities as physical exercise, yoga, dieting, or programs to quit smoking. While private-sector organizations can generally place higher restrictions on unhealthy activities, government can influence behaviors by, for example, passing laws to restrict smoking in public places and to limit the sale of foods high in trans fats, which raise levels of bad cholesterol (LDL) and lower levels of good cholesterol (HDL).

Healthy living involves eating good food and maintaining a proper weight, exercising regularly, limiting the consumption of alcoholic beverages, avoiding the use of tobacco and illegal drugs, and getting regular physical checkups. Following these steps can reduce the use of sick time and increase a person's energy, strength, stamina, and mental well-being.

It almost seems too obvious that these few steps to healthy living can make such a dramatic difference in the probability of a person's living a long, productive life, yet many people make poor decisions that adversely affect their health and well-being. One reason is, of course, the addictive properties of tobacco, drugs, and certain foods, and poor habits taken up early in life are difficult to break.

Special Programs

Special programs provide assistance to targeted workers or groups. Affirmative action programs assist women, minority group members, and disabled workers in finding employment opportunities, while an employee assistance program (EAP) helps workers with special problems navigate through their difficulties before their work performance is negatively affected.

ENABLING OPPORTUNITIES

Not everyone has the same opportunity to go to college or attend the best universities, nor does everyone have the same access to job opportunities. Still, many opportunities are available that we might not recognize or take advantage of. How we approach these opportunities or respond to them can influence our career development.

Approaches and Responses to Enabling Opportunities

How do we approach and respond to enabling opportunities? Do we actively pursue opportunities and take advantage of them? Do we cheerfully accept opportunities when presented? Or do we resist or sabotage opportunities? Clearly, people approach and respond to opportunities very differently. Three factors affect the way we approach opportunities: (1) the value we place on ourselves, (2) the value we place on the opportunity, and (3) the fit between our aspirations and opportunities.

When a person places a high value on herself, she may be more confident about taking on new opportunities and more enterprising in entering into new educational programs, new assignments, and new organizations and networks. On the other hand, she may be somewhat cavalier toward opportunities, refusing to pursue avenues she feels are below her skills or capabilities. When a person places a low value on herself, she may be less willing to venture forth into new opportunities, fearing failure and disappointment. The concept of self-efficacy, which is addressed in Chapter 4, pertains not only to the effort a person puts into her job, but also to the effort she puts into pursuing self-development opportunities.

When a person places a high value on opportunities, she will presumably seek them out, try to learn more about them, and consider a wide range of choices. In addition, she will not burn bridges, being more likely to leave doors of opportunity open for future consideration by building networks and relationships. When a person places a low value on opportunities, she may be less interested in pursuing them and more willing to close doors. It can be a fatal career mistake.

When a person places a high value on having a good fit between herself and opportunities, she may be more selective and less flexible. Selectivity can work out well when the person is able to get the job she always wanted, but very often there are trade-offs for being too selective, such as remaining in a job with a lower salary or job benefits. Moreover, many highly selective people never get the job they want or must wait many years before an opening becomes available. Still, a bad fit is almost certain to result in disappointment, so a person should give careful thought when considering that next job opportunity and how well the job fits her aspirations.

Types of Opportunities

While some opportunities can be "purchased," be obtained through networking, or become available under special programs, some opportunities are illicit or even false if the proposed benefits are misrepresented, are misinterpreted, or disappear. Still, most opportunities are achieved the old-fashioned way: they are earned.

Purchased opportunities are obtained by direct or indirect payments. Employment opportunities can be "purchased" in the sense that someone who can afford a good education will have better employment opportunities. And a person with financial resources may have the opportunity to create her own business or buy into an existing business. She can also accept employment opportunities that do not pay a high salary but will ultimately lead to career advancement, an option not available to the person living day-to-day constrained by her inability to relocate, her transportation options, or her childcare needs.

Opportunities through networking are available in high schools and colleges by joining clubs, committees, and special projects. Professional associations, community and alumni organizations, and political parties also provide broad opportunities to network that can lead to job opportunities. Learning the art of building networks and nurturing relationships is also good preparation for organizational leadership.

Generally, clubs, organizations, and associations require effort and commitment above and beyond normal schoolwork or job requirements, so a person must learn to work more efficiently in order to get everything done—an additional benefit that is noticed and appreciated. On the other hand, over-commitment and failure to accomplish expected work can send the opposite message of being unreliable or even incompetent, so learning one's limits in order to make wise choices is another valuable lesson.

Affirmative action programs provide special employment and educational opportunities for women, minorities, and disabled persons. While there is a general range of opportunities provided to people in American society and some people do have better opportunities than others, there have been periods in the history of our country where some groups, most notably women, African Americans, and American Indians, were systematically denied access to opportunities.

The Civil Rights Act of 1964 outlined protections against discrimination with the goal of providing equal rights and opportunities to minorities. The Supreme Court recently affirmed the legality of programs to increase minority representation based on a long history of inequality, but suggested these programs could some day be voided if true equal opportunity can be achieved.

Special enabling opportunities for the underprivileged might involve training programs or employment arranged by social service agencies. Special opportunities are also provided for gifted and talented students. Once employed, an individual can benefit from mentoring programs that help new employees navigate their new work environment and leadership development programs for employees targeted as future leaders in the organization.

Illicit opportunities—ranging from cronyism to benefits from sexual favors—are illegal or at least violate social norms or standards. Because quid pro quos can be used to improperly open doors to opportunities, there are codes of conduct that set out limitations on accepting gifts, using public resources or inside information, and engaging in inappropriate office relationships. The underground economy is predicated on the illicit activities of providing services below the market value by not claiming earned income and evading taxes and Social Security payments. The practice of employing immigrants who entered the United States illegally shows how an illicit opportunity that began as a minor event can evolve into a major social dilemma.

False opportunities can be the result of misrepresentation by an educational institution or employer, or they can occur from one's own self-deception, misperception, or lack of information. Often, a person will think she is headed in the right direction but has misinterpreted working conditions or terms of employment or has failed to perform fact-finding about an organization.

A student might be awarded a degree without receiving adequate education, or she might be led to believe her degree will lead to a promising career, while the actual prospects for employment are poor. Once on the job, a person might be led to believe she is in line for a promotion, when a decision has already been made to promote someone else.

Ultimately, most opportunities are earned. While people complain about special privileges of the rich and famous, unscrupulous employers benefiting from illicit opportunities, or special opportunities for certain people or groups, even people in these situations must prove themselves once in the educational program or on the job. An opportunity is a door, not a guarantee.

Most successful organizations place a high value on their staff and invest heavily in employee development; they place a high value on providing developmental opportunities and a range of assignments for their employees; and they place a high value on having a good fit between a person and her job. While some opportunities may be purchased, or obtained from networking or special programs, ultimately opportunities must be earned. Organizations need to be wary about succumbing to illicit or false opportunities that may ultimately place them at legal risk or create distrust among workers.

Not all doors to educational opportunities are open to everyone. But neither do all opportunities depend on only the financial condition of the individual or her family. There are many ways to open doors to opportunities—prepare for opportunities through research and planning, set goals and identify how to achieve them, and seek opportunities and recognize them when they appear.

When opportunities arise, step forward and embrace them. Show gratitude to those who help along the way, and be diligent about not burning bridges. Often, setting the groundwork leads to future opportunities, so be careful to treat everyone with respect because the person slighted today may be the best resource for a new opportunity tomorrow.

SELECTED LITERATURE REVIEW

This section presents a sample training program evaluation and a brief discussion on current training issues, trends, and programs.

Sample Training Program Evaluation

Ammons and Niedzielski-Eichner (1985) offer a practical framework for evaluating supervisory training programs in local government. The authors interviewed 12 of the 14 recipients of the Clarence E. Ridley In-Service Training Award presented by the International City Management Association (ICMA) between 1969 and 1982 and 60 of 81 members of the American Society for Training and Development (ASTD). All 12 of the ICMA award recipients and 83 percent of the ASTD members reported participating in a coordinated management/supervisory training program of some kind.

The authors created an evaluation grid for a management development-supervisory training program by matching four levels of evaluation—reaction, learning, behavior, and results—against 14 performance areas—effective performance appraisal, interpersonal communication, decision-making/problem-solving, basic supervisory skills, team building, productivity improvement methods, human behavior skills, general office procedures, stress management, time management, budget process, written communication, achievement of subordinate performance/accountability, and public relations.

Ammons and Niedzielski-Eichner posed a key question for each of the four levels of evaluation:

- Level 1 (Reaction): Are trainees satisfied with the training provided?

- Level 2 (Learning): Did the trainees learn the information/concepts introduced?

- Level 3 (Behavior): Is the information/concept used by the trainee on the job?

- Level 4 (Results): How does the application of the information/concept affect the organization?

At Level 1 (Reaction), trainees identify how satisfied they are with the training program through the use of a survey. At Level 2 (Learning), they are tested on what they learned. At Level 3 (Behavior), their behaviors are evaluated predominantly by the use of a survey. At Level 4 (Results), results are measured by comparing pre-training measures to post-training measures or by post-training interviews or reviews.

Ammons and Niedzielski-Eichner concluded that an effective training evaluation system is valuable, but for various reasons, relatively few local governments in 1985 were involved in systematic evaluation of their training programs beyond the reaction level.

Training Issues, Trends, and Programs

Today, two decades after the study by Ammons and Niedzielski-Eich-ner, evaluations of training programs have come a long way. Salas and Cannon-Bowers (2001) note that many theoretical frameworks and models were developed over the previous decade that address the design and delivery of training, and they conclude that because there is extensive use of technical evaluation tools to assess training services against outcomes, training is no longer without a theoretical base.

Salas and Cannon-Bowers observe that a critical part of training in the new work environment is organizational and job/task analysis, which provides congruence between training goals and organizational goals. Training addresses both the cognitive and behavioral aspects of job performance, and the antecedents to training include cognitive ability, self-efficacy, goal orientation, and training motivation. They go on to discuss training methods and instructional strategies involving tools, methods, and content. In particular, they note the use of technology for video conferences, online/Internet training, and simulation-based training and games, predicting a growing role of technology in training.

Salas and Cannon-Bowers further note that researchers have investigated how learning can be optimized through feedback, practice, and reinforcement schedules. They also discuss the works of those who have used stress-exposure training (SET), where trainees are given preparatory information on stressors followed by behavioral and cognitive skills training, and simulated events to practice what they learned (Salas and Cannon-Bowers 2001; Driskell and Johnston 1998; Johnston and Cannon-Bowers 1996). They conclude with discussions about training evaluation and applying the knowledge, skills, and abilities (KSAs) acquired from training to actual job performance.

The WPF describes enablers as a critical part of the theoretical structure of HR systems. This literature review presents an example of a sophisticated evaluation tool for training programs and a number of contemporary lines of inquiry in training and development.

ENABLING PROGRAMS

Several HR enabling programs align with the HR service objective of meeting the employee development needs of the organization and the HR strategic objective to build HR capacity. Enabling programs include traineeships, training programs, and mandatory and discretionary training programs.

Traineeships

Traineeships are generally used to fill positions that cannot be filled at the journey level, either because there are insufficiently qualified candidates or because the job requires special on-the-job training and development. Traineeships are also useful for transitioning clerical or paraprofessional staff to professional or technical positions. These employees may have worked on assignments where they learned many of the agency's operational procedures and demonstrated initiative to do more than their jobs required.

While their counterparts from outside the organization would receive training on the agency's operational procedures during a traineeship, these support staff are trained only on the technical or professional competencies that one would otherwise obtain in a college or trade school. In some cases, employees can obtain relevant degrees and credentials that allow them to take a "transition" examination so they are not required to compete with the general population. These opportunities are important because they allow the organization to retain good workers who might otherwise be laid off as a result of computerization or leave the organization once they have acquired new credentials.

Training Programs

Training programs generally address four areas: (1) traineeships; (2) training programs carried out by an agency or contracted out, including programs that address recent updates or changes in policies, procedures, equipment, or software programs; (3) educational programs at colleges, universities, or professional societies; and (4) on-the-job training (OJT). While OJT can involve formal training goals and timetables, too often the supervisor is not adequately prepared to serve as a trainer, so OJT can be a hit-or-miss proposition. If a supervisor is a very good trainer, she will be highly valued and often assigned more new workers than average.

Mandatory and Discretionary Training Programs

In the WPF, there are various types of mandatory and discretionary enabling opportunities, and intranet resources support or augment these opportunities. Figure 3-2 divides mandatory enabling opportunities into six categories of participants: new hires, new supervisors, new managers, professionals, all staff, and targeted staff. While Ammons and Niedzielski-Eichner described how supervisory and management development programs were important for ICMA award winners, not all organizations win awards or provide this training. Figure 3-2 challenges the HR manager to determine whether mandatory training for these various sub-groups exists, or if not, whether it should be developed.

FIGURE 3-2 Sample Organizational Enabling Opportunities

Mandatory	
Target Audience	*Enabling Instruments*
New Hires	*Orientation* *Traineeships* *Guidance: Mentoring, Coaching*
New Supervisors	*Supervisory Training* *Labor Relations Training* *Time and Attendance Training*
New Managers	*Management Training* *Leadership Training* *Performance Measurement Training*
Professionals	*Continuing Education Credits*
All Staff	*Legal and Policy Training* Discrimination Sexual Harassment Ethics Privacy and Confidentiality
Targeted Staff	*Retraining* Technology New Procedures *Counseling* Employee Assistance Disciplinary

Discretionary	
Target Audience	*Enabling Instruments*
Targeted Staff	*Education* Coursework toward Degree *Professional Associations* Conferences Seminars Continuing Education Credits *Technology Training* *Health and Fitness Programs* *Employee Assistance Programs* *Other Special Assistance Programs*

Intranet Resources	
Target Audience	*Enabling Instruments*
All Staff	*General Administrative Resources* *New Hire Resources* *Supervisory Resources* *Managerial Resources* *All Employee Resources* *Discretionary Resources* *Opportunities* Job Openings Special Assignments Volunteer Activities

For the new hire, it is rather obvious that an orientation is needed, but do the organization's new hires mostly learn their job by OJT, or are they required to complete a set of structured training modules? Is there a tracking system that monitors the progress of all new hires, or do the program managers dismiss structured training because there is too much "real work" to be done? Are new hires assigned a mentor or coach to guide them in understanding the organization, or is guidance provided haphazardly, if at all?

For the new supervisor, are supervisory training, labor relations training, and time-and-attendance training mandatory at the time of promotion or even prior to promotion, or are they made available only whenever the organization or new supervisor gets around to them, if at all?

Are new managers given training on management, leadership, and performance measures at the time of appointment to a managerial position, prior to appointment, at everyone's convenience, or not at all? Is managerial training mandatory? Is it tracked? What are the consequences?

Presumably, every new hire, new supervisor, and new manager should receive training within a short time of her new work assignment, if not prior to the assignment. This allows the organization to be confident that the worker is fully enabled and can be held accountable for her performance. Mandatory training can also include continuing educational credits for professional staff who are required to maintain licenses or special credentials. The HR manager must track this information, even when the organization does not reimburse staff for the costs.

Training on laws, regulations, and agency policies such as discrimination, sexual harassment, ethics, and confidentiality is generally mandatory for all staff. In cases where charges are brought against an individual and the organization, training records are valuable for reducing or eliminating organizational liability by showing the employee was trained on the prohibitions against certain acts and the consequences of violations.

This information is also useful when the organization acts to discipline or terminate an employee for improper activity.

Mandatory training might also include retraining for targeted staff on changes in procedures due to new technology, training on new work assignments as a result of redeployment, sessions related to disciplinary actions, or counseling on employee assistance programs. While counseling on employee assistance programs might be considered a mandatory activity, actual participation in an EAP is generally discretionary, unless it is a part of a disciplinary agreement.

Discretionary training includes courses taken toward an educational degree, professional association activities, technology education, health and fitness training, employee assistance programs, and other special assistance programs.

An organization's intranet can provide useful resources to augment training activities. Other enablers such as job openings, special assignments, and volunteer work can be posted on the intranet to let all employees know what opportunities are available.

Implementing Training Programs

In determining whether training is mandatory or discretionary, the HR manager should understand that all mandatory training must be tracked and completed within an established time period. If managerial training is needed for all new managers, it should be provided as soon as possible—presumably within one year of appointment. The completion rate needs to be tracked and reported, and low completion rates must be increased. Online training courses can be created to ensure that people have the opportunity to complete the training on time.

Some information might be critical for staff to know but is not provided in a formal training course. Even when a training course is provided, information is often forgotten or not completely understood until a worker goes through a situation where she actually needs to use it. Therefore, the HR manager must provide ways, in addition to online training, for workers to access information at the time they need it. Checklists, "how-to" guides, frequently asked questions (FAQs), and reminders can all play a part in enabling the worker.

An intranet library of resources may be a solution, but maintaining and updating it can be a problem. Thus it is important to place ownership of materials on specific people who are accountable for keeping the information current. Sometimes, the best suggestion for getting the right information at the right time is to simply identify a contact person whose name is posted on the intranet.

KEY PERFORMANCE MEASURES

Chapter 2 presented sample efficiency measures for the task of filling positions in the organization. Table 3-1 lists hypothetical key measures for employee development. The table includes two sets of efficiency measures—production and backlog—and one effectiveness measure—attendee ratings of training programs.

TABLE 3-1 Sample Employee Development Measures

	Mandatory					Discretionary
	New Hires	New Supervisors	New Managers	New Training	All Employees	All Employees
Number of Employees	150	125	125	2500	2500	2500
Production						
Average Number of Staff Trained Each Year 2004–6	120	120	100	2200	2340	700
Staff Trained 2007	125	115	100	2220	2360	800
Change	5	−5	0	20	20	100

TABLE 3-1 Sample Employee Development Measures

	Mandatory					Discretionary
	New Hires	New Supervisors	New Managers	New Training	All Employees	All Employees
Training Targets	**150**	**125**	**125**	**2500**	**2500**	**1000**
2004–2006 Average Participation Rate vs. Target	80%	96%	80%	88%	94%	70%
2007 Participation Rate vs. Target	83%	92%	80%	89%	94%	80%
Percent Change	3%	−4%	0%	1%	1%	10%
Backlog of Requests for Training Events						
Start of 2007	3	5	2	6	16	75
End of 2007	4	4	5	4	17	90
Change	1	−1	3	−2	1	15
Average Rating by Attendee (Scale of 7)						
2004–2006	5.7	5.1	5.8	5.8	5.8	5.7
2007	5.9	5	5.7	5.9	5.9	5.9
Change	0.2	−0.1	−0.1	0.1	0.1	0.2
Percent Change	4%	−2%	−2%	2%	2%	4%
Rating Targets	**6**	**6**	**6**	**6**	**6**	**6**
2007 vs. Target	−0.1	−1.0	−0.3	−0.1	−0.1	−0.1

Under production, the table shows the number of people in each subset and the number who received training. This allows a manager to calculate participation rates. In those cases where participation was mandatory, the training target is 100 percent. When mandatory targets are not met, the organization needs to take corrective action.

Where the training is discretionary, the organization can use baseline information from 2004–06 to get targets for future participation rates and can use interventions to increase participation. For example, the HR manager might survey staff to see what discretionary employee development activities are of interest to them and increase participation rates by providing the most popular activities. Another option is to make participation in certain programs mandatory.

Using backlog information, the HR manager can determine whether the requests for training are important and obtainable. She then must prioritize and schedule, placing the most critical training first. Because the mandatory training is more important than discretionary training, it is obvious why we report the largest backlog is in discretionary training.

HR managers can use attendance ratings to evaluate trainer effectiveness. Low results might mean that certain instructors should not be used in the future, or perhaps the content needs to be revised. There should be clear expectations that these ratings will improve over time by learning from survey feedback and making changes.

Training production, backlogs, and attendee ratings help explain whether employee capacity has increased during the designated period. Training performance measures compared to targets show the HR manager whether she is meeting the training needs of the organization. Comparing performance measures for training to organizational performance measures indicates whether better training performance contributed to better organizational performance.

While Table 3-1 provides measures on overall mandatory and discretionary employee development activities, further data mining is needed for the various categories listed in Figure 3-2, "Sample Organizational Enabling Opportunities." Individual training sessions can be evaluated to determine which areas did the most for building capacity that translated to improved performance.

THE FUTURE STATE OF HUMAN RESOURCE MANAGEMENT AND RESEARCH OPPORTUNITIES

The selected literature presented earlier in this chapter is not exhaustive, but it does bring to light helpful information. The work of Ammons and Niedzielski-Eichner provides a good example of the value of training and ways to measure that value. Salas and Cannon-Bowers show how far training has come in the areas of evaluation, research, and practice. Still, there are significant opportunities for future research.

It is important to expand the concepts of training and employee development to encompass the goal of enabling the worker. This broader view includes providing opportunities for staff growth and encompasses EAPs, affirmative action programs, and other programs that provide special assistance to targeted groups. Future research on ways to train people to be more opportunistic could lead to more effective employee development and human services programs.

Studies are already under way on benchmarking enabling services. As these benchmarks become better known and become more credible from a growing a body of evidence, the role of training will become more valued. The need for increased training in today's workplace is evident by the regular upgrade of computer equipment and software, and the constant changes in the workplace resulting from new technology. Another important research opportunity involves exploring the most responsive methods for providing important training and information to workers at the time when they need it.

WHAT MAKES A GOOD WORKER?

General mental abilities and personality traits strongly influence whether a new worker will become a valued employee. Among the personality traits with strong correlations to job success are integrity and conscientiousness, while extroverts make more outgoing, friendly, and optimistic workers. Staffing concerns must also expand to include the physical and mental health and well-being of prospective workers and respond to their socioeconomic conditions. In the public service, we must be proactive not only in improving performance, but also in our outreach efforts.

From the vantage point of employee growth and development, it is clear that a person who is interested in gaining new skills, learning new information, and becoming more technologically proficient will be more successful in a new work environment than someone who resists change and shows no interest in learning. The valued worker is someone who participates as a volunteer and gets to know people in a less formal setting within the organization. She seeks out special assignments and projects to gain a variety of skills and at the same time gets to know her coworkers and build relationships. The most effective worker not only pursues self-development but also helps others develop by being a mentor or coach, a skilled supervisor or manager, or simply a guiding coworker.

For people who are not aware of growth expectations and opportunities, the organization must provide guidance to help them realize their potential, so they can become better workers.

HR programs and services are vital to meeting today's organizational challenges and embracing future organizational opportunities. An important tool for building HR capacity is employee development. Employee development goes beyond training to the broader goal of enabling the worker, including giving her opportunities to gain experience. Moreover, new KSAs are constantly required in the evolving workplace.

Ultimately, performance measures of the organization's employee-development activities must show whether these programs are building, or at least sustaining, HR capacity, and they must contribute to overall organization performance. These measures should lead to rewards and celebrations for successes, as well as point the way to corrective actions for addressing shortcomings.

PART 2

Performing the Work

Work Inputs:
The Cause of Everything

I n the Work Performance Framework (WPF), work inputs are the cause of everything. Phrasing it that way is only a slight exaggeration, for in the cause-effect relationships of the work environment, all causes that can be attributed to people can be described as inputs.

This chapter first discusses the three types of work inputs within the WPF: competencies, effort, and power. Then it presents a selected literature review on the topics of causation and data analysis to explain how inputs meet the conditions required for attributing causation. The chapter next discusses HR programs that build performance by building work inputs and examines key performance measures for these programs. The chapter concludes with some thoughts on opportunities for future research.

WORK INPUTS IN THE WORK PERFORMANCE FRAMEWORK

In classical use of general systems theory, inputs are presented as resources that include raw materials, people, financial resources, and capital. These resources go into a black box described as processes and come out of the black box as outputs. This mental image is easy to imagine when we think of the ingredients in a cake going through a process that involves assembling the ingredients and placing them in the oven. In a short time the ingredients, or inputs, come out as a cake, the output.

General systems theory in the WPF and applied to human resource management is somewhat different. The role of a person as a resource is somewhat more difficult to imagine, since he does not go into the oven or come out as a cake. Instead, the person must use his ability to bake a cake in order for the process to be completed. His contribution is not as an ingredient but rather as the baker.

People are not instantly ready to be a resource; rather, they must be prepared to serve as a resource. This preparation involves staffing, or selecting the people with the best general mental abilities and personality traits, and enabling them to act as a human resource—in this example, as the baker.

Fully prepared human resources are workers who apply competencies, effort, and power to complete work by transforming raw materials and other resources into outputs. See Figure 4-1, which describes these three categories for people functioning as work inputs.

FIGURE 4-1 Work Performance Framework—Work Inputs

Work Inputs	Components
Competencies	Professional
Knowledge	Technical
Skills	Operational
Abilities	Administrative
	Managerial
	Supervisory
	Writing
	Computation
	Computer
	Reasoning
	Oral
	Interpersonal

Work Inputs	Components
Effort Intention Energy	Self-Discipline Self-Efficacy Willingness Initiative Perseverance Stamina Strength
Power Authority Resources Influence	Decision-making Communication Relationships

Competencies

Knowledge, skills, and abilities (KSAs) are the terms generally used to describe the mental and physical abilities needed for people to perform work. More recently, the term *competencies* has been used in place of KSAs, but this term has also been linked to behaviors. The WPF views behaviors as processes, not inputs. Often, competencies are considered to be personal attributes or personality traits such as honesty, integrity, and conscientiousness. The WPF presents competencies as applied abilities and classifies them as inputs, while personality traits are potential abilities and categorized as human resources.

The use of the term *ability* here is general in nature, suggesting that one is capable of being trained (potential ability) or able to actually do the work (applied ability). The term *knowledge* involves understanding and retaining information, while the term *skills* usually suggests a physical aspect of work such as the competency needed by a skilled machinist or a skilled typist. Abilities involve applying knowledge or skills to various types of mental or physical activities such as reasoning, communicating, or performing calculations.

Sometimes it may seem difficult to distinguish between a knowledge, skill, or ability. For example, computer skills can mean the physical adeptness or dexterity to move the curser about the screen using a keyboard and a mouse, whereas computer knowledge might mean knowing the different functions on the tool bar, but we usually look for a person to have the greater ability to both understand and use the computer hardware and software effectively.

This author developed a list of several general KSA categories that was used in developing civil service examinations:

- Professional or technical

- Operational

- Administrative, managerial, and supervisory

- Writing and computation

- Computer

- Reasoning and decision-making

- Oral presentation

- Customer service and interpersonal relationships.

Examples of professional or technical competencies include a thorough knowledge of electrical engineering, or a thorough knowledge of grounds maintenance, including turf, trees, and shrubs. The first example describes an entire profession, whereas the second example presents a subset of knowledge required to perform more specific tasks and activities.

Operational KSAs include knowledge of the laws, rules, regulations, policies, procedures, and manuals that apply to a particular government agency. Supervisory, managerial, and administrative KSAs pertain to the additional responsibilities of supervising staff, managing programs or projects, or working on administrative activities such as personnel and budgeting.

Writing ability is important for work in the public sector because public administrators are required to prepare numerous written reports and develop very precise and complex regulations and policies. Computational abilities are required for performing complex mathematical operations and computations, and for developing tables and spreadsheets.

Computer KSAs can range from the typing skills required to type a document using a desktop computer to being able to use standard software or write programs. A position identified as business analyst or business systems analyst requires the ability to analyze information and systems by working with computer and program experts to develop computerized processes that make work more efficient or effective within professional, technical, or operational standards. Since government agencies provide a great deal of information to many customers and stakeholders, computer programming and business systems analysis have been at the center of major productivity gains.

Reasoning, decision-making, oral presentation, customer service, and interpersonal relationships are the remaining categories of competencies often evaluated by civil service examinations in the form of oral tests. In the WPF these attributes are linked to the effective use of power, and they are discussed later in the chapter.

Customer service competencies are critical to call-center operations, where customer service representatives are on the telephone all day assisting people seeking answers to specific, but often recurring, questions. In this setting, the worker must understand how to be polite and courteous to the caller, help the caller identify the specific information or answer she is looking for, answer the caller's questions, and when necessary, refer the caller to another, more appropriate worker. These competencies now extend beyond the call center as the concept of customer has broadened to include all people seeking services.

In Chapter 2, competencies were linked to civil service examinations. In Chapter 5, competencies will be linked to position classification, including the allocation of salary grade.

Effort

Effort is the second aspect of people functioning as work inputs in the WPF. Since effort is closely related to motivation, it is useful to look first at the topic of motivation, which is an antecedent to work performance. While effort addresses how hard a worker actually worked, motivation speculates how likely a person is to work hard based on such factors as interest in the work, rewards, and feelings of affiliation to his employer and coworkers.

Motivation

Motivation addresses three basic questions:

- When establishing and pursuing goals, what do I want or need?
- What is the probability of obtaining my goal and related rewards?
- How will I best attain my goal?

The first question addresses quality-of-life issues; the latter two address efficiency.

The first question—"When establishing and pursuing goals, what do I want or need?"—is addressed in motivational literature under needs and values. Needs are associated with our emotions and our terminal values or what we want out of life. Chapter 8 discusses emotional reaction as an impact in the WPF. Satisfied needs can lead to fulfillment, while needs that are not satisfied can lead to longings; motivation can be driven by past fulfillments or longings.

The second question—"What is the probability of obtaining my goal and related rewards?"—is addressed in motivational literature by two prominent theories. The first theory, self-efficacy, seeks to determine the variation in effort based on the variation in the perceived probability of completing an assignment. Interestingly, researchers have noted that while someone with low self-efficacy might give a low amount of effort because of the perceived likelihood of failure, someone with very high self-efficacy might also apply low effort because of complacency (Latham and Pinder, 2005; Vancouver, et al., 2001). Self-efficacy also involves contextual issues related to work and whether the person believes there will be a good person-to-job fit.

The second theory, expectancy theory, seeks to determine the variation in effort based on the variation in the perceived probability of being properly rewarded for completing work. This theory is directly related to the real and perceived validity of civil service examinations that are used to promote workers and to the concept of fairness. When promotion examinations do not accurately rank candidates on the basis of their work performance, workers may become complacent about how well they work. (The concepts of rewards and fairness are discussed in Chapter 7 as a part of work outcomes.)

The third question—"How will I best attain my goal?"—involves strategies for achieving success. This line of inquiry holds constant a person's values, needs, and perceptions about the likelihood of success and looks at personality traits as the variable that explains how people will attain their goals. Latham and Pinder (2005) note that extroversion, conscientiousness, tenacity, core self-evaluations, goal orientation, and strategies for self-monitoring and self-regulation are among the topics most discussed.

The core activity linking these personality traits to motivation is goal setting. Self-regulation involves setting goals and seeking feedback in order to regulate one's activities (Latham and Pinder 2005; Latham and Locke 1991). Self-monitoring involves overseeing one's behaviors to create and sustain a positive image in the workplace. Conscientiousness relates to working hard and being reliable. Tenacity and passion have been studied as factors of entrepreneurialism (Latham and Pinder 2005; Baum and Locke 2004). The "high performance cycle" motivational theory proposes that high goals lead to high performance, which in turn leads to high rewards and new high goals (Latham and Pinder 2005; Latham et al. 2002).

The challenge in looking at motivation in relation to effort is to differentiate those aspects of motivation that apply to inputs from the ones that apply to outcomes and impacts. The concepts of self-discipline, self-efficacy, and goal setting were gathered from the literature on motivation and integrated into the explanation of effort within the WPF.

Intention

In the WPF, effort is divided into two general areas: intention and energy. Intention is presented as having five levels: (1) self-discipline, (2) self-efficacy, 3) willingness, (4) initiative, and (5) perseverance. (See Figure 4-1.)

Basic self-discipline means following acceptable work standards, such as working at a reasonable pace, coming to work on time, and treating people respectfully. Self-efficacy involves a person deciding whether he is capable of performing the work. In making this determination, he must decide whether he *can* do the work and whether he *wants* to do the work, i.e., whether there is a good person-to-job fit.

Willingness suggests that a person intends to do a good job. Willingness presupposes that the person understands the job requirements and the likely outcomes, which according to expectancy theory include rewards, obligations, and possible adversities that may come with the position. Sometimes, however, a person accepts a job before carefully examining important aspects of his self-discipline, self-efficacy, and work expectations, resulting in a premature or weak decision, and he may find that he is incompatible with his new job. When the job does not work out, the employer has wasted resources and the worker has wasted his time, so theories about self-monitoring, self-regulation, self-efficacy, and work expectations are important from the vantage point of both the organization and the individual.

Initiative is a proactive intention to set goals. The person with initiative seeks to explore new opportunities and avenues for achievements rather than just to complete the work he finds in his in-basket. Goal-orientation theory distinguishes learning goals, which involve self-development and growth, from work performance goals. Self-monitoring, self-regulation, and more advanced aspects of self-discipline enable a person to be aware of how he is perceived in the organization, monitor his behaviors, focus on those aspects of work that align with his individual goals, and stay on track to achieve them. On a cautionary note, when personal goals are incompatible with organizational goals, problems can arise, and self-enhancing goals may be harmful to group performance (Latham and Pinder 2005; Seijts and Latham 2000).

Perseverance is the persistence to continue in the face of adversities. Adversities include time ("Will I have to sacrifice my private time if I take on more work and responsibility in the office?"), personality conflicts, risks associated with failure or financial loss, greater work demands, and general uncertainty. Courage is perseverance in the face of danger. Perseverance does not necessarily mean confrontation or assertiveness, although these strategies cannot always be ruled out. Part of perseverance is understanding adversities and knowing how to deal with them. Perseverance involves having the strength to deal with difficult situations, learning strategies to reduce adversities or disarm them, wanting goals enough to endure quality-of-life trade-offs, and earning the respect of others by being remarkably successful.

Adversities do not appear as prominently as one might expect in the motivational literature. We can easily imagine the role adversity plays when taking on a new job or assignment. While a person might think he can do the work and will be well rewarded, he might decide to turn down a promotion because he doesn't want the hassle that comes with the opportunity. Often, people decline promotions when the job changes from doing their own work to overseeing the work of others.

Energy

Although a person may have the strongest intentions to be successful, as the saying goes, "The road to hell is paved with good intentions." Once a person has developed strategies to maximize his intentions, he must still have the energy to act on those intentions and see them through. The WPF presents energy as two capacities—strength and stamina—that apply to both mental and physical energy. Strength refers to the energy available at a critical moment, while stamina refers to continuous energy.

Zohar et al. (2003) describe energy as a limited resource, which when stretched beyond its limits might lead to emotional and occupational problems. They note that occupational stress occurs when coping resources are insufficient to match job demands. These stressors might involve role conflict or ambiguity, and work overload; job demands that are not accompanied by sufficient authority to act; and job demands that conflict with family demands. Eventually, stress can lead to exhaustion of energy and professional burnout. The Zohar study noted that unexpected, stressful events and workload led to negative emotional reactions and depleted energy following the event and at the end of the day. They also reported that the enhancement of meeting a goal mitigated these negative results at the time of the event, and actually restored energy levels by the end of the day.

These findings in the Zohar study fit well within the WPF. The job demands of role conflicts and work overload are among the list of adversities presented in the WPF. While there may be a limit to an individual's energy, there are strategies that can be implemented to manage energy exertion. For example, an organization can establish rules on acceptable behaviors to manage personality conflicts. Yeo and Neal (2004) report that the relationship between effort and performance increased with practice; it follows, therefore, that practice dealing with various types of adversities will reduce ambiguity and energy loss and increase effectiveness and efficiency.

Finally, although cognitive abilities do correlate with work performance, a great amount of the variation in job performance is unexplained by test score differences. This suggests that (1) the range of cognitive variation in the pool of candidates for many jobs might not be as high as presumed by the literature; (2) the range of energy capacity in the pool might be larger than suggested; or (3) energy strategies might play a larger role than presumed, particularly in dealing with adversities.

It is important to note that adversity is often intentional and used as a tool for power. A powerful person might be abusive to staff by speaking in an offensive way or requiring work to be completed within an abbreviated time period. A subordinate can also create adversity by being difficult or sabotaging his superior in a vulnerable or highly public situation. Part of energy strategy is to deal effectively with intentional adversity used to challenge one's authority and power and not be drained of energy assets, which can result in stress and sleepless nights. Still, sometimes intentional adversity cannot be overcome, and a person chooses to move on to another job. Often, his predecessor made the same decision.

Clearly, physical fitness also affects stamina. Unfortunately, when we are short of time because of work demands, we often leave our physical fitness and health unattended. This neglect is particularly a problem when we use food or alcohol as a reward for working hard or to relieve our stress. Building energy capacity through physical fitness is not just important to success; it also improves our quality of life.

Power

The third area of HR inputs is power. A person can have the necessary competencies, strong intentions, and lots of energy, but if he does not have the power to act, the other attributes may be thwarted. He might have a great idea to improve a product, but if he does not have the power to act, the idea will never be realized. Figure 4-1 presents power in terms of authority, resources, and influence. Power is having the authority to act, the access to resources needed to complete work, and the capacity to influence others.

Authority

The first indicator of authority is the person's title because it represents his role in the organization. The head of an organization is the ultimate authority for that organization. The middle manager has some authority but is subordinate to the head of the organization and higher-level managers. Entry-level staff have the least authority to act, and that authority is based on the duties and responsibilities of the position. But authority is not a constant because part of authority is determined by how it is used. If a person has authority but does not use it, for all practical purposes he has no authority. If a person assumes authority he does not have, and good things happen, he might well gain credibility and have *de facto* authority.

The head of an organization holds total authority to decide who gets appointed, selected, or terminated, although in the public service there are often constraints to hiring and to firing people at will, i.e., without cause or due process. Along with this authority, the head of the organization has full access to the organization's resources. He also has responsibility for managing the agency's greatest challenges, including its overall performance, working with other government agencies to acquire their support, and obtaining outside resources.

When an organization is large, the agency head must delegate authority to subordinate staff. Often, a new agency head brings in his political team to ensure trust and reliability, and to reward those who have helped him achieve success. Authority is further delegated down the hierarchy to middle managers, who are not generally politically appointed. No matter how much authority is delegated, however, the head of the organization is still responsible for agency outcomes, and he will be the one criticized for his agency's poor performance. Sometimes, this can lead to a strategy of avoiding problems rather than achieving results.

The middle manager, who has been delegated some authority, is accountable to the higher managers in the organization, but he too must delegate authority well to achieve satisfactory results and avoid problems. At the same time, he must maintain good relationships with his higher-level managers.

Entry-level staff have the least amount of authority to appoint people, delegate work, or have direct access to agency resources. Entry-level staff with a narrow perspective may well focus on completing the work they are assigned but neglect establishing and maintaining relationships with their peers and superiors. However, people with initiative who are seeking to advance in the organization understand the dynamics of power and authority and recognize the importance of managing relationships.

Resources

When preparing a budget, financial administrators allocate revenues to maintain or build organizational resources, including human resources, financial resources, and capital. Resources play a critical role in power.

Just as a person who is extremely competent and motivated may be thwarted by a lack of authority to act, he may also be thwarted by a lack of resources. At the highest level, the leader and high-level managers must allocate resources effectively and efficiently to maximize productivity and build a strong, cohesive organization.

The mid-level manager must also allocate resources effectively, generally concentrating on operational goals. At the same time, he might need to appeal to higher managers for additional discretionary resources to accomplish new goals. At the entry level, staff must use the resources they are given with limited opportunities to request more. Project managers who work on temporary assignments or develop new programs for the organization have a particular need to identify the resources required to achieve their goals.

Financial resources are also essential for managing work, in part to reward productive workers. When financial rewards are tied to salary grades and job titles and not to performance, a critical part of managerial power is restricted. When promotions are tied to civil service examinations with low validity, these financial rewards are restricted even further. Prior to the civil service reforms of the 19th century, the public service was marked by political abuse of financial resources, so just handing over all agency resources to the leadership without constraints is unacceptable. An accurate performance assessment system and allocation of financial rewards based on performance are essential outcomes for the high-performance organization. (This issue is discussed in more detail in Chapter 7.)

Influence

While a leader can have sufficient authority and access to resources, he must also have the capacity to influence others. This capacity is closely tied to effort and competencies. Influencing others can be strenuous work.

Just as an energetic leader can be very influential, a leader with little energy can deflate an entire organization.

The competencies that most relate to influence are (1) the ability to reason clearly and make sound decisions; (2) the ability to communicate with people and make oral presentations; and (3) the ability to establish interpersonal relationships. Not surprisingly, these are the competencies that were most often evaluated by oral tests at the New York State Department of Civil Service.

We influence other people by communicating with them, both verbally and nonverbally, and by building interpersonal relationships with other workers, customers, and stakeholders. It is easy to see how the personality traits of extroversion, agreeableness, openness to experience, and emotional stability are related to communication and establishing interpersonal relations. It is also easy to see how conscientiousness is related to establishing relationships within a work environment. We can also imagine that people deficient in these areas are less likely to be good managers and leaders.

Wild and Kerr (1984) provide an example of targeted training to enhance communication and interpersonal skills. In their study, they provided students with influence training to be applied in a job interview. The treatment group was provided four days of training on persuasion, including the elements of attractiveness, expertness, and trustworthiness. The control group was trained on transactional analysis. All students then underwent a simulated job interview for a summer camp job in which they were instructed to persuade the interviewer that he or she was the right person for the job.

The results showed that those who had received training in persuasion were significantly more successful than those who had received no training. While innate personality traits are important in communication and interpersonal skills, these skills can be improved through training. (More information on communication and interpersonal relations is presented in subsequent chapters. Chapter 5 discusses work behaviors as a work process, and Chapter 6 discusses interpersonal communication as the output of work behaviors.)

Perhaps the most important aspects of power are reasoning and decision-making. The person who makes no decisions has no power, and the person who makes bad decisions risks losing his power. Although decision-making is a competency and a work input, the best decisions are made with an understanding of the full WPF. While decision-making is presented here as a cause, its full value is presented in Chapter 8 in connection with intellectual impact.

SELECTED LITERATURE REVIEW

Although different work environments may generate different results, the capacity of people to affect their work performance is accounted for in the WPF by just three factors—competencies, effort, and power. The selected literature review for this chapter explores the concept of causation as it relates to work inputs.

Causation

All science is based on the establishment of cause-effect relationships. We know that winter weather in New York State gets very cold, and why. The angle of the sun and the amount of sunshine vary in the course of a year because Earth rotates around the sun on an axis that is not quite perpendicular to its orbit. Because we have less sunlight in the winter, and the sunlight does not hit us as directly, we have colder weather. If only we could explain work performance as simply, so we could develop measurement instruments that perfectly predict how much work a person we are about to hire will actually do!

Public administration and personnel administration are social sciences, and our measurement instruments are not nearly as precise as meteorology. A common explanation for the low predictive powers of measurement instruments in the social sciences is that people are not machines: we are too complex to be explained, and we have free will, so we can choose not to do something. Nonetheless, arguments are being raised in the public administration and HR literature about the need for better scientific techniques and analyses. Three areas of data analysis are particularly relevant to these arguments for improving the scientific study of people and behaviors: latent variables, attribution of cause, and data supply.

Latent Variables

When a measurement instrument such as a civil service examination produces a validity coefficient (R) of .35 and accounts for just 12 percent of the variation (R^2) in work performance, the obvious question is: What accounts for the other 88 percent? One answer is latent variables, i.e., concealed variables that are unknown, unmeasured, or unobserved. Another explanation is omitted variables. These are known variables that might be immeasurable or too difficult or expensive to measure, or simply not used. For example, the Scholastic Aptitude Test (SAT) was found to under-predict the performance of women attending college. Key omitted variables were identified as the number of hours studying and the percentage of readings and other assignments completed (Sackett et al. 2003; Stricker et al. 1993). A challenge for the WPF is to account for omitted or missing variables that affect individual work performance.

Attribution of Cause

Gill and Meier (2000) note that causality generally means that when X changes, Y will subsequently change, but when Y changes, X will not change in any predictable way. For example, if I hammered a nail into the wall, I caused the nail to go into the wall, and the nail would have no reverse cause on me or the hammer.

Meier and Brudney (1997) assert that four conditions must be met to establish the existence of a cause-effect relationship. First, there must be time order—the cause must precede the effect. Second, there must be covariation, so that if one (cause) occurs, the other (effect) must also occur. Third, the events cannot be explained by a third factor, or as Meier and Brudney explain, the events must be nonspurious. Finally, there must be an underlying theory to explain the relationship.

Thus, consistent with the rule of time order, the hammer's coming down on the nail preceded the nail's going into the wall. Consistent with covariation, the nail went into the wall when receiving the force of the hammer. Consistent with the rule of nonspurious events, the nail going into the wall cannot be explained by any other reason than the force of the hammer driving it into the wall.

Historically, causes of human activities have been difficult to isolate, and cause associated with covariation often appears to work in both directions. For example, does a great leader make great workers, or do great workers make a great leader? Here, cause appears to move in both directions—a great leader must have great workers, and great workers must have a great leader. We also experience excuses like "I would have done the work, but my car broke down." Thus unpredictable events affect work performance.

Bollen (2002) identifies two ways to evaluate latent variables and attribute cause—*a priori* analysis and *a posteriori* analysis. While *a priori* analysis predicts what will be, *a posteriori* analysis evaluates existing data to attribute cause after the fact, provided a substantial amount of data has been gathered. While we may not be able to predict when a car will break down, we can, after the fact, evaluate how many times unforeseen events interrupted work, and factor these unforeseeable events into our work schedule. This process may not totally eliminate the problem of latent variables, but it certainly helps us manage work.

While past practice may not be a perfect predictor of future events, it is a useful source of information to make predictions, and a look back after an event can produce insights into planning future events.

Data Supply

Gill and Meier (2000) lay out a manifesto for public administration research and practice—that public administration needs to develop a data archive. They maintain that "public administration differs from other fields and professions in that it lacks core data sets that comprise the basic data infrastructure for the field" (159). In the realm of HR management and civil service examinations, in particular, the relatively low validity of civil service examinations has thwarted the development and sharing of data, especially to the general public and to the general population of public service managers and administrators.

Early construction of the WPF began by *a posteriori* analysis of the data from performance assessments administered between 1990 and 1995, when recurring activities were found for the best performers. These activities include managing or working in highly productive programs and special projects, providing good customer service to both internal and external customers, pursuing improvements and innovations in work processes and systems, and pursuing staff and self-development. The first three sets of activities became the bases for the three work processes in the WPF (covered in the next chapter), while the fourth set became the basis for the enablers discussed in the previous chapter.

The question remained, What causes high performance? Historically, the answer given by the HR community has been knowledge, skills, abilities, and personal attributes. The people who had the KSAs to do the work and the appropriate personal attributes would be the most productive workers. Unfortunately, the low validity of civil service examinations, which measure KSAs, suggests that KSAs do not provide an adequate explanation. Moreover, when personal attributes were presented as personality traits and personality tests such as integrity tests were added to the examination, the results, while somewhat better, still fell far short of the target of producing eligible lists with high enough validity to ensure that the best performers could be appointed or promoted.

What are the missing variables? The first missing variable identified in the WPF is effort. Just as SAT scores are insufficient to predict college success because some students, particularly women, study longer and complete more assignments, many people who score lower on civil service examinations work longer and harder than many of their higher scoring coworkers. This still left a missing variable because we often see smart, hard-working people not getting promoted for legitimate reasons. This led to the conclusion that power is the other missing variable as a cause of work performance. Within the construction of the WPF, these three variables—KSAs, effort, and power—are presented as inputs.

Thus the WPF proposes that these variables—competencies, effort, and power—taken together meet the causal conditions set forth by Meier and Brudney: (1) time order, that is, these inputs precede the effects, which are work results; (2) there exists covariation, so that if these inputs occur, the work results must also occur; and (3) the events are nonspurious, that is, the sequence of events cannot be explained by any other variable, latent or omitted. The WPF provides the underlying theory to explain the relationships.

HUMAN RESOURCE PROGRAMS TO MANAGE INPUTS

At the input stage of the WPF, the worker has been hired and is being paid to work, so the organization must now manage his work performance. Individual performance is managed using probation evaluations and performance evaluations, while group performance is managed on a larger scale through performance management programs. Time and attendance sheets prevent leave abuses, which can be a problem affecting efficiency and performance. For the HR manager, the key strategic question is, Is this organization building HR performance? Or is performance remaining the same or even decreasing?

Probation Evaluations

Once appointed, a worker begins his career as a probationer. The probationary period provides the organization the opportunity to evaluate a worker's performance and, if dissatisfied, to terminate his employment relatively easily. While a problematic worker must be given reasons for termination, he does not generally have the right to an administrative appeal. In New York State the probationary period can be completed any time between 26 and 52 weeks of service. If a probationer's performance is unsatisfactory, he can be terminated after just eight weeks; however, a probationer has appeal rights if his service is terminated before he has worked eight weeks, since he must be provided a fair and reasonable opportunity to do well.

Traineeships often last up to two years; in these cases the probationary term coincides with the traineeship. New York State requires a probationary period for promotions as well; if the performance is unsatisfactory, the probationer is returned to his lower level position.

During the probationary period the supervisor must evaluate whether the new worker is performing well and learning the job at an acceptable rate. At the end of the probationary period, the organization must decide whether to retain the employee. This is no small decision. Consider that an employee making $50,000 a year for 30 years will receive $1.5 million over a career; with benefits, the amount could total $2.25 million or more.

This is obviously a very conservative estimate because it does not take into account inflation and cost-of-living increases. Nonetheless, it is easy to appreciate that early development can have a compounding effect on the return of the HR investment, and that termination during the probation period is an important tool to cut investment losses.

Lingering doubts about a probationer's performance might very well prompt an organization to decide to terminate him. Once tenure is granted in the public service upon successful completion of probation, an employee gains substantial protections against termination thereafter. Thus the probationary period is an important stage, and a supervisor not only must be a good trainer but also must be able to make difficult decisions that have a profound effect on the organization and the new employee.

The first-line supervisor is often the person who is given this responsibility, but he may be ill-equipped to handle the assignment. He may be newly appointed himself without a great deal of experience; he may be close to the same age as the new employee or perhaps younger; or he may have gone into his career wanting to do technical work, without any interest in overseeing someone else's work.

New employees often have very high aspirations but limited experience, and personality conflicts can arise between the supervisor and his new employee when they have different opinions about what constitutes satisfactory performance. Therefore, the organization must be keenly aware of these operational risks, and take proper steps to address them by making sure new employees and new supervisors are afforded proper guidance.

Part of this guidance comes from a sound orientation program for new workers that lays out the values and expectations of the organization. This orientation should explain the mission and goals of the organization and identify performance pitfalls, such as unethical and discriminatory behaviors that will lead to disciplinary actions. The organization must be sure that the supervisor has explained the specific work performance expectations to the new employee, consistent with the duties of the position, the vision and mission of the agency, and the organization's work culture and work climate.

The importance of the role of the supervisor in the new employee's initial employment cannot be overemphasized. Supervisory training on dealing with personality conflicts, coaching and mentoring techniques, and other supervisory activities is critical to both building HR capacity by helping the new employee in his development and building HR performance by setting out clear, consistent work expectations and monitoring performance.

As will be discussed later, the supervisor should also be well versed in how to "build community" with the new worker, showing interest and respect by understanding and appreciating his concerns, values, and interests; providing mentoring and coaching, including introducing the new worker to the organization's networks; and providing a breadth of work assignments.

Performance Evaluations

After the probationary period has been completed, periodic performance evaluations that assess the employee's performance and development must be completed. A key part of the evaluation is setting goals for the employee's future development. Once again, a new supervisor may be unsure of himself in evaluating the performance of another person, while the employee may not be comfortable being evaluated.

Some might claim that performance evaluations are counterproductive, meaningless, and ineffective, and there is evidence that performance evaluations are often subjective. Criticisms in a worker's performance evaluation can be taken very personally, and resentments can develop when the employee perceives that his supervisor is painting an unfavorable public picture that could harm opportunities for advancement or promotion. Sometimes, workers believe that their work cannot be evaluated because they are not providing direct services involving measurable work outputs. As a result, performance evaluations are often reduced to brief discussions, or simple ratings of satisfactory or unsatisfactory.

Despite the criticisms and misgivings, probation evaluations and performance evaluations are extremely important to the organization because they directly address the strategic questions about how well the organization is managing its human resources. The solution is not to abandon the evaluation process, but to do it better.

Performance Management

While probation evaluations and performance evaluations are tools for a supervisor to evaluate the development and work performance of his subordinates, the information from these reports is also critical to the larger picture of the organization's overall progress in building HR capacity and HR performance. Top managers need accurate information on staff development to make adjustments to employee recruitment and development programs, and they need accurate information on staff performance to correct performance deficiencies and expand successes.

Managers use employee development and performance results to decide which employees should be placed in critical positions throughout the agency in order to grow new programs, fix existing programs, or replace managers who retire. During this process, particular individuals may be placed on temporary assignments or projects to develop a broader picture of the organization's operations, bringing them into contact with other managers and key staff.

Often, the organization expects that when the temporary project becomes a permanent program, the temporary project director will become the new program director. The organization also uses staff performance and development information in succession planning when certain employees are selected for special leadership or management programs in preparation for future high-level appointments.

Time and Attendance Sheets

Time and attendance sheets are used to track attendance and use of leave credits. While there are legitimate uses of sick leave and protections for persons with disabilities, abuse of sick leave is a problem that affects efficiency and performance. The new employee needs to understand the legitimate uses of leave credits, and the new supervisor needs to know how to identify and track abuses. The program manager and the organization's leadership must have access to time and attendance records and data that create a picture of the organization, identifying pockets of leave abuses and any correlations to problems in overall work production and performance.

KEY PERFORMANCE MEASURES

Most promotions are made by using eligible lists established as the result of civil service examinations. The most common method to evaluate workers' competencies is a written test in which a matrix of competencies is constructed and candidates are given a sufficient number of questions to ensure representation. Oral tests are often used for higher-level positions, particularly those involving managerial activities. More recently, written tests that simulate work experiences and track the candidate's process of solving management problems have been used.

Figure 4-2 is a sample survey of indicators of reasoning, decision-making, communicating, and building interpersonal relationships. This survey was used in a study (Southworth 2000) to evaluate the reliability of oral test ratings. The study involved 13 oral tests and 199 candidates. With three raters for each oral test, the study included nearly 600 ratings to analyze. The standard oral test calls for raters to give preliminary scores, discuss the candidate's performance among themselves, and then award their final ratings. Concerns had been raised whether the discussion violated the independence of the panel members' judgments and affected their ratings, particularly where there might be a strong, persuasive panel member. In the study, raters were asked to complete the questionnaire presented in Figure 4-2 prior to discussing their preliminary ratings. The rest of the rating process was unchanged.

FIGURE 4-2 Sample Persuasion Measures

Questionnaire Instructions				

Please indicate the extent to which you agree or disagree with each of the following descriptions of knowledge, skills, and abilities. Use the scale below and write the number which best represents your answer in the space next to each item.

To what extent do you agree with the following statements about the oral test candidate?

Strongly Agree	Somewhat Agree	Neither Agree Nor Disagree	Somewhat Disagree	Strongly Disagree
1	2	3	4	5

Factor I – An Ability to Reason Clearly and Make Sound Judgments

I.A Problem Solving

_____ Demonstrates an understanding of the problem situation; identifies existing or potential issues; recognizes conflicting information

_____ Carries out problem-solving procedures—identifies problem, researches the situation, identifies possible causes and solutions, selects solution, and evaluates results

I.B Work Processing – Planning, Implementation, and Evaluation

_____ When planning activities, identifies priorities and recognizes constraints

_____ Articulates resources necessary to achieve goals; in assigning work, considers staff experience, performance capabilities, and schedules; assesses in-house limitations and contacts outside parties as necessary

_____ Monitors progress of assignments; ensures that planned activities are completed within a reasonable time

_____ Identifies steps to evaluate the effectiveness of workload; measures productivity

I.C Program Expertise

_____ Demonstrates breadth of viewpoint; demonstrates an alertness to problems' implications and soundness and relevance of solutions

_____ Ensures that resources are allocated to high-impact areas

_____ Ensures that workers are held responsible and accountable for complying with professional standards and legal requirements

_____ Uses cost-benefit and cost-effectiveness analyses and other evaluative techniques

Factor II – An Ability to Present Ideas Clearly and Effectively

II.A Communication Abilities

_____ Presents ideas clearly, concisely, and accurately

_____ Makes thorough, logical, and well-organized presentations

_____ Responds to follow-up questions directly and completely

_____ Uses appropriate diction, grammar, and vocabulary

II.B Persuasion

_____ Through communication skills and efficient and effective activities, builds support for agency programs

_____ Recognizes and addresses other perspectives

_____ Displays interest and enthusiasm; conveys a sense of importance for the issue being discussed

_____ Demonstrates ease of discussion; effectively uses gestures and facial expressions

II.C Conflict Management

_____ Deals with conflicts among staff or between staff and customers/constituents appropriately

_____ Where possible, assumes a solution orientation; attempts to bring about a lasting solution by addressing underlying causes

_____ When necessary, asserts authority and/or managerial role

_____ Recognizes importance of face-saving strategies

Factor III – Ability to Establish Satisfactory Relationships with Others

III.A Leadership

_____ Demonstrates poise, self-confidence, ease of interaction, and decisiveness

_____ Demonstrates an ability to motivate staff and provide necessary direction, leadership, and guidance; formulates major planning priorities using a team approach and provides guidance to subordinates in prioritizing and planning their priorities

_____ Instills in staff the necessity for objectivity, rational findings, thoroughness, and accuracy, and employs sound professional judgment in the development of agency reports and documents

_____ Procures necessary resources and manages resources to maximize efficiency and effectiveness

III.B Team Building

_____ Displays an orientation toward achievement

_____ Establishes effective work relations; uses team skills in the workplace to lessen the rigidity of the organization and focuses on common goals and plans; affords staff appropriate leeway and delegates work effectively; uses others in problem identification, analysis, and solutions

_____ Notifies upper management of critical issues such as potential time overruns and any need for changes in the focus of approved work plans

_____ Shows concern and respect for others; displays friendliness and humor

III.C Staff Development

_____ Delegates work effectively; shares information with staff and listens to them; shares credit with staff

_____ Identifies training needs of staff and allocates appropriate resources

_____ Conducts and oversees a performance evaluation process designed to inform employees of what they have done well, in what areas they need to improve their performance, and with the objective of developing employees for greater responsibility in their role in the organization

_____ Demonstrates sensitivity to staff member stress, personal problems, and/or need for professional development; articulates criticisms in a constructive manner

The study compared the survey results to the final oral test ratings, generating correlation coefficients of .84 for the individual survey results and oral test ratings and .94 for the composite survey results and oral test ratings—results that supported the hypothesis that raters do act independently. Their judgments were consistent with one another, generating an average inter-rater reliability of .96 for the oral test ratings for the 13 oral tests. The survey form also generated a very high internal reliability (Alpha=.96), which suggests that a survey format might be useful as an alternative to narrative oral test rating sheets or for employment interviews. The form can also be readily adapted to a performance evaluation process.

Key performance measures for effort could be constructed by addressing the two components identified in the WPF for effort: intention and energy. A scaled evaluation for intention could be set up as follows:

- Level 1 Effort: Demonstrates self-discipline

- Level 2 Effort: Demonstrates self-efficacy

- Level 3 Effort: Demonstrates willingness

- Level 4 Effort: Demonstrates initiative

- Level 5 Effort: Demonstrates perseverance

Energy is implied in "demonstrates," so levels of energy could be distinguished by using such terms as "seldom," "often," "regularly," and "always."

Another set of key measures for probationary evaluations and performance evaluations can be adapted from the performance assessment documents presented in Chapter 7. Performance assessments can be used to conclude that a worker has provided high work input by evaluating his staff and self-development activities, work accomplishments, customer service and interpersonal activities, and contributions to the organization's successful improvements and innovations.

THE FUTURE STATE OF HUMAN RESOURCE MANAGEMENT AND RESEARCH OPPORTUNITIES

The research literature on input measures concentrates on competencies, or the KSAs required to perform work. While motivation is also a prominent part of the research literature involving work performance, the WPF proposes that effort is a better representation of work inputs. Moreover, power is presented in the WPF as a third type of HR input.

In the WPF, effort is important to performance, but how much effort should a person give to his job? While effort can vary greatly among workers, there must also be a concern for just how much time and effort people should be expected to give to their jobs. Zohar et al. (2003) explain that when job demands are very high, worker fatigue and stress can occur. While energy may vary significantly between workers, it is not an unlimited commodity.

It is also important to be concerned about employer expectations—e.g., a common expectation that people should give their entire lives to their jobs to get ahead. Job descriptions that limit work assignments and unions that seek to grieve out-of-title work assignments often undermine the aspirations of the hard worker to excel, but how much effort should a worker give? This question will undoubtedly be at the center of attention in the future as employers seek to achieve higher levels of program performance and at the same time control labor costs.

The construction of work inputs in the WPF provides numerous avenues for research. We hope the research community will move beyond competencies to study effort and power as the possible missing variables of work inputs, and in so doing, confirm the contents of the WPF. At the same time, research is needed to evaluate the upper limits of energy and the social costs of demanding so much from workers that quality of life and well-being deteriorate.

The elements of work inputs within the WPF are (1) competencies or applied abilities; (2) effort, including intention and energy; and (3) power, which involves having the authority to act, the resources needed to get the work done, and the capacity to influence other people. Work inputs are presented as the cause of all worker job performance, which makes them central in understanding the framework and the field of HR management.

This chapter also provides insights into the differences between the antecedents to work performance covered in Chapters 1 and 2 and the actual causes of work performance. These are important insights that may well transcend the field of HR management into other social sciences and even the physical sciences. An oft-repeated saying among researchers is that correlation does not necessarily indicate causation. In essence, this means that although there might be covariation between events, it is often unclear which event, if either, is the cause of the other event. While researchers have tried to unravel the distinction, the WPF provides a clear delineation between the antecedents of work performance and the causes of work performance.

Chapter 5 discusses work processes in the areas of work production, work behaviors, and work improvements and innovations, reveals how different competencies are needed for the different work processes, and describes how high productivity and other contributions to the organization can be achieved in different ways.

Work Processes: How the Work Gets Done

n this chapter the discussion turns from work inputs to work processes—the systems and procedures for accomplishing work and
producing outputs. Position classification is used to identify the
common activities for a group of positions with the same title, while
job analysis links competencies to the critical activities. To understand
what inputs are needed, we must understand what activities are to be
performed. This chapter takes a global view of work processes as the next
part of the Work Performance Framework (WPF).

The chapter begins with background information on the role of work
processes in the WPF, breaking down work processes into three areas:
work production, work behaviors, and work improvements and innovations. Next, the chapter presents a selected literature review on conflict
management, a key challenge for managing work behaviors. It continues
with a discussion of HR programs that address work processes, and it
presents key performance measurements for classification activities. The
chapter concludes with a discussion of important issues related to the
future of HR management and research opportunities related to work
processes.

WORK PROCESSES IN THE WORK PERFORMANCE FRAMEWORK

Work processes are divided into three areas: work production, work behaviors, and improvements/innovations. (See Figure 5-1.)

FIGURE 5-1 Work Performance Framework—Work Processes

Work Processes	Components	Standards
Work Production Direct services Administration Infrastructure Support	*Produce* *Control* *Maintain*	Standards of Correctness Repeatability Quality Assurance
Work Behaviors	*Oral Communication* *Written Communication* *Demeanor* *Gifts*	Self-monitoring
Work Improvements and Innovations	*Invent* *Design* *Create* *Test* *Implement* *Monitor* *Correct*	Change

Work production involves the core duties, activities, and tasks typically included in a duties description. In the public sector, the outputs of work production are generally services, rather than products. In public-sector HR management, core HR services include classifying positions, providing program managers with lists of qualified candidates, and processing personnel transactions that formally change a worker's employment status (e.g., a new job title, a different salary grade).

Work behaviors are separated into a different set of work processes because they provide a different output from services—interpersonal communication. Thus, if an organization is undergoing a reduction in force, the HR manager must carefully communicate concern for those workers who must be separated from the agency and assure the remaining workers that the worst is over, to limit the breakdown in workers' trust and affiliation with the organization.

Work improvements and innovations—short-term or long-term initiatives to increase productivity and foster better work behaviors—are separated from work production because they also provide a different output—new, improved, or simply more efficient work processes, systems, and outputs. For example, if workers became disillusioned with the organization during a prior down-sizing episode, the HR manager might decide to hold a series of small group sessions prior to or following the next set of layoffs, to let the workers vent their feelings and help calm their anxieties.

Work Production

Work production involves the work processes for producing core outputs (services). A work production system has two aspects: direct services and indirect services. Workers involved with direct-service activities interact with the customers or stakeholders. Indirect services include administration—acquiring and managing the resources needed to conduct business through personnel activities, budgeting, and reporting—and infrastructure support—operations that support direct-service and administrative activities (e.g., maintaining buildings and equipment, maintaining and upgrading technology, updating service procedures and operations manuals, developing and revising service policies).

Work production is guided by three principles: standards of correctness, repeatability, and quality controls. These tenets suggest that there are a limited number of effective ways to complete a task; that once identified, these best procedures can be repeated; and that with quality assurance controls in place, output quality can be maximized. Professional standards and laws provide the starting point for work standards and correctness, while rules, regulations, policies, and procedures established by the organization refine the standards and laws.

The computer and its ability to record data have brought special challenges to managing work production. Organizations are now required to continuously improve by tracking and measuring service performance, which results in shifting production goals. Therefore, high-performance and acceptable standards today will probably seem like average-service performance in the future as goals change, processes evolve, and expectations increase.

For example, one change felt in many public-sector organizations today is the growing demand for access to public records under the Freedom of Information Act. Records that are maintained electronically can be transmitted instantaneously, so the public and media want immediate access to them. This places a burden on the public-sector organization, particularly when timeframes are set for the release of public records. Often, public records must be edited and information redacted, so organizations argue that the data does not exist in the form requested. In the future, however, we can imagine that public organizations will be required to maintain records subject to public disclosure in a format that accommodates quick release. This will dramatically increase the transparency of public-sector operations.

Work Behaviors

Work behaviors are the interpersonal or behavioral aspects of work performance. The output of work behaviors is interpersonal communication. The purpose of work behaviors is to establish affiliation and trust with customers and coworkers by establishing a relationship, which might be as brief as a single interaction or could last for many years. Work behaviors that create favorable relationships enhance the appeal of the individual worker and the organization.

Forms of Work Behavior

Work behaviors are presented in the form of oral or written communication, demeanor or nonverbal communication, and gift giving. Oral communication can often be more effective than written communication because of the variety of communication techniques one can use, but it is short-lived and can be forgotten or overlooked when a mistake is made or a wrong message is sent. Written communication is more likely to be a permanent record, and written correspondence can be more precise because it is often edited for content and tone at several levels in the organization, depending on the sensitivity and importance of the message and the recipient.

A conversation or a letter must do more than simply address a request for service or information; it must also communicate to the recipient a tone and sensitivity to demonstrate that the request or topic is legitimate and the recipient is important, thus establishing trust and affiliation. Of course, sometimes a correspondent will overdo a matter that has been carefully reviewed and evaluated, so the written communication must bring the matter to a close while still being respectful.

For example, a person who has appealed her ratings on a civil-service examination may not be pleased with the administrative decision to dismiss the appeal. She might write a letter to the head of the agency that conducted the administrative review, to provide additional arguments or complain that certain facts were not properly weighed. A response to her complaints should explain that the administrative-appeal process has ended and that any complaints should have been presented in the appeal and cannot subsequently be considered.

Demeanor, or nonverbal communication, also transmits messages to a recipient about trust and affiliation. While someone might "turn his back" or "give a cold shoulder," much nonverbal communication is transmitted by facial expressions. Russell et al. (2003) discuss vocal and facial expressions of emotions, which include anger, laughter, smiling, sadness, and fear. They note that emotional expressions are sometimes interpreted incorrectly or presented as a deception, and can at times be unwelcome.

Meanwhile, a "cool" demeanor can send a message of distance and lack of concern. Because of the broad range of interactions among workers or with customers or stakeholders, the best behavior will vary, depending on the circumstances. Nonetheless, the skill of establishing good interpersonal relationships is highly valued, and demeanor often plays an important role. The previous chapter noted that interpersonal skills are key to being able to persuade others, and persuasion is a key element of power.

Gift giving can be a very effective work behavior to build trust and affiliation. Celebrating birthdays and other special occasions can be viewed as an act of warmth, especially when the gifts are thoughtful and carry special meaning for the recipient. Usually a financial limit is placed on gifts in the public sector to avoid conflicts of interest, and there are other potential dangers associated with gift giving, including unwelcome gifts and jealousies from a third party.

Adverse Conditions

The previous discussion on behaviors to promote good relationships with coworkers and customers assumes a stable work environment. But what about adverse situations, when people display confrontational or negative behaviors? Can we and should we still act the same way, or should we adopt different behaviors?

There are many devices for working through conflicts or negotiating a solution when a customer or coworker is creating a dispute. Although the vocal and facial expressions of the disputant might be displaying anger, as noted earlier such displays are not always interpreted correctly and may be presented as a deception or tool to elicit a strong reaction from the worker. It is important in these situations for the manager to not display her own emotions in a way that escalates the problem. At the same time she must act firmly and not be intimidated. When the dispute becomes intractable, there are established procedures for dealing with a difficult person, and when the situation is believed to be dangerous, the proper authorities need to be brought in immediately.

Uncooperative or difficult staff can pose many problems for a supervisor. Disciplinary procedures are used to address work production problems related to time and attendance, failure to accomplish assigned tasks on time, or failure to meet quality standards. But when conflicts develop over time and lead to a lack of trust, respect, or affiliation, disciplinary procedures may not provide an answer.

The first solution is often to reassign the subordinate. While such actions might be viewed as an indictment against the subordinate, the supervisor might be viewed as ineffective in building a team environment and passed over for future for promotions when conflicts with subordinates are repeated. Because of tenure protections in the public sector, termination is not always available as an alternative for workers with poor attitudes so long as they do their work, but problem behaviors can go on for many years and contribute to a poor work environment or staff turnover. Thus work behaviors that develop trust and affiliation are important to work performance.

Conflicts may go beyond a supervisor and her subordinate. In a hierarchical organization, problems associated with work behaviors often increase as a person rises in the organization. As she gains experience in dealing with adversities and conflicts at the lower levels, she becomes more adept and better prepared to face the more difficult challenges.

This scheme is confounded somewhat in a team or project work environment where workers from various parts and levels of the organization are brought together to solve specific problems or take on specific initiatives. Newer team members may have had limited opportunities to deal with adversities and develop strategies to address them.

Ilgen et al. (2004) identify the importance of group activities related to such issues as trusting, bonding (affiliation), helping, and learning. Because team members may be unfamiliar with the appropriate behaviors to build trust and affiliation, meetings are increasingly carried out under standardized behaviors using protocols for managing meeting time, encouraging participation, and respecting the comments and ideas of all members.

Top-level managers, politicians, the courts, and the press operate in a special environment of power where intimidation is often used as a tool. Information and communication must adhere to the strictest of protocols; time is of the essence; and the consequences of mistakes can be enormous. Trust and affiliation may prove to be a more difficult challenge, and different attributes such as character and articulateness may achieve greater bonds than warmth and consideration. In this environment, a person's demeanor must, above all, reveal strength. People who show weakness, incompetence, or verbosity are closely scrutinized.

Negative Behaviors

Is it useful at times to use negative behaviors? It appears that some very effective managers operate with an iron fist or a nasty temper. Can negative behaviors actually build trust and affiliation? Because we often look at these leaders as role models, these are important questions.

To address this issue, we need to distinguish between negative work behaviors, punishment, and anger. As already noted, positive work behaviors are a tool for building trust and affiliation. Negative work behaviors, on the other hand, include overt and covert acts of sabotage or disrespect to a stakeholder, customer, or coworker, and are intended to diminish trust and affiliation.

While rewards are positive outcomes for doing good work, punishment is a negative outcome in response to poor work performance. Because work production is continuous, punishments (and rewards) can be given on a regular basis and not necessarily just at the end of a work production cycle. A punishment can be given for failing to complete a required course (enabling), low effort (work input), falling behind on an assignment (work process), or poor service (work output). Consequently, a punishment, if communicated poorly, can be perceived as a negative work behavior that diminishes trust and affiliation. Similarly, a reward (a work outcome for a work accomplishment) can be perceived as a gift (work behavior to build trust and affiliation) when given early in the work production cycle.

Anger, moods, and emotions are other pieces of the work behavior puzzle. While it might be desirable for a person to demonstrate energetic passion toward her work and the people in her organization, the negative emotional reaction of anger might surface when work is not going well. Brief and Weiss (2002) distinguish moods, which are a generalized state, from emotions, which are associated with specific events or occurrences. While positive emotional reactions can be joyous and jubilant, negative emotional reactions or responses may bring about anger or tears, depending on the propensity to dominate or withdraw.

Anger, particularly when it is directed at a specific person, can be very upsetting and threatening to people within earshot. On the other hand, an outburst might be interpreted as an emotional display by someone who is passionate about her work and wants badly to succeed. While anger is tolerated occasionally when circumstances are extremely stressful from work or from stressors outside the workplace, anger does not promote trust and affiliation, nor is it an appropriate form of punishment.

Yelling can be a form of anger, an act of intimidation, or simply a tool to get someone's attention. Yelling "No!" to a child about to touch a hot stove is no doubt appropriate, and we see coaches yelling at football players. A raised voice, which is milder than yelling, is a useful tool to assert a person's role as a leader or her position on an issue. However, as previously mentioned, expressions of emotions are often unwelcome and can be interpreted incorrectly or presented as a deception. Whether someone raises her voice or yells as a tool to assert her position or ideas or as an emotional expression of anger, it is clearly subject to misinterpretation and might be viewed as harassment by an unappreciative listener.

Work behaviors in the WPF are narrowly construed as the work processes for providing interpersonal communication. This narrow interpretation points out the distinction between work behaviors and rewards and punishment, and it brings into question the use of certain emotional expressions and devices that might appear harsh or negative.

Standards of Behavior

Standards of correctness, repeatability, and quality control and assurance mechanisms can be established for work behaviors just as for work production. Trust is established, in part, through behaviors that adhere to standards of correctness including respect and fair treatment and, in part, through behaviors that communicate consistency and reliability. Affiliation is achieved by understanding and relating to the emotions and values of coworkers, customers, and stakeholders. (Chapter 8 provides an extensive discussion on emotional impacts that are tied to affiliation as well as judgmental and attitudinal impacts that are tied to trust.) Because we have different preferences, we relate to people differently. Still, some people are clearly better than others at establishing interpersonal relationships, and some behaviors are clearly harmful to building relationships and need to be avoided.

Quality control and assurance for work behaviors are generally out-lined in an organization's administration manual and address topics such as using leave credits, reporting time and attendance, and prohibiting dis-crimination and sexual harassment. Recently, e-mail communications in the workplace have come under close scrutiny for improper tone, content, or sensitivity. Work e-mails do not enjoy the privacy protections of home e-mails. Because organizations can be held liable for the actions of their employees, e-mail training has become more common, and an inappro-priate e-mail can bring swift disciplinary action, even termination.

Other protocols designed to protect the security of computer systems prohibit visiting banned websites and downloading documents or pic-tures. Should litigation occur, standards and quality controls for work behaviors can limit an organization's exposure to risk by demonstrating to the court that a harmful action perpetrated by an employee was pro-hibited by the organization.

Quality control and assurance for some improper work behaviors are carried out indirectly and harshly. Subtle controls include failure to get resources and loss of career opportunities. Work behaviors are very important processes in accomplishing work, and effective work behav-iors can magnify performance, while negative behaviors can diminish perceptions of work accomplishments.

Work Improvements and Innovations

Work improvements and innovations are included in the third category of work processes in the WPF, and these processes have been largely cred-ited with the continuous increases in productivity over the last several decades. These dramatic gains are highly leveraged by advances in com-puterization, telecommunication, and the improved ability to manage, manipulate, and analyze information. The importance of the new role of managing information systems is evident by the presence of an information resources management component of administrative services in virtually every large organization.

A number of work improvements have occurred as a result of the advances in managing communication and information. Timeframes of distribution systems have been shortened to just-in-time, in order to minimize inventories. Meetings are often held by conference calls and videoconferences, eliminating travel time and costs. Hand-held communication devices enable people to manage activities and relations from anywhere. Where once paper transactions were manually completed and distributed by mail, there are now electronic transactions. Computers calculate financial transactions, dissect information into innumerable reports, and electronically audit financial systems. Typing mistakes are eliminated by backspacing or automatically corrected by word-processing programs. Computers even fix many of their own problems automatically.

Customer service call centers have been designed and redesigned with scripted responses and recorded messages that efficiently lead the caller to the appropriate answers to her questions. Improvements have also been made to the customer's interpersonal experience by using protocols of pleasantness and respect.

New work processes have been developed to bring about these innovations and improvements, and questions about how to improve services or innovate are constantly raised. Who needs the information, and when do they need it? Can a computer do the work? Does the work need to be done at a specific location? How should we train the users of the new systems? Can the Internet be used to make information and services available to the customer and answer her frequently asked questions? How long will it take to build the system or make the changes, and how much will it cost? Raised expectations now lead to demands for further improvements and even better services.

Most production outputs for the public sector are services rather than products, so most outputs of improvements and innovations are better, faster, and cheaper services, information, and systems. These improvements and innovations come largely from advances in computerization and telecommunications. Many improvements are made by outside vendors whose products have broad application and can be adapted to different public-sector organizations. At the program or operational level, standard procedures are evolving to make continuous computer and telecommunications systems improvements through system conversions, system upgrades, and in-house improvements.

Stages of Improvement and Innovation

The stages for making improvements and innovations are invent, design, create, test, implement, monitor, and correct—with the first stage, invent, being unique to innovations. For computer system conversions and upgrades, a committee consisting of outside vendor representatives and in-house staff is typically set up. Initially, these committees were viewed as temporary special projects; however, for larger systems where there are almost continuous upgrades and in-house improvements, a committee may become permanent, and some project members may be involved with their assignments on a full-time basis for many years.

During the design stage, project managers and assistants work with program staff to identify the steps for providing services and processing information by developing work flow charts. The sequencing of events is laid out; decision points are identified; and work paths are created for each possible decision.

The system conversion, or upgrade, is then created from the work-flow analysis, and the system or subsystems are tested to see whether the process has correctly incorporated all the possible steps and decisions. Once the tests have been completed, the system is placed online for actual work, and the program staff is trained on the procedures for using the new or revised system. System performance is monitored, and errors are identified and corrected.

Because systems are built in progressive stages, early errors have a compounding, negative effect on costs, so undetected errors made at the design stage can dramatically multiply the costs to correct the errors by the time the system has been brought online. An industry rule is that a problem that takes one hour to correct at the design stage takes ten hours to correct if undetected until after the system has been constructed and 100 hours to correct if undetected until after the system has been fully tested and implemented. Thus the earliest stages have come to be recognized as the most critical.

The position of business systems analyst has evolved in recent years as a key figure in the systems development process. The business systems analyst works with the program staff to help them understand technology features, and with the technology staff to help them understand the business process requirements.

Work Improvements

Just as standardized procedures have evolved for implementing system conversions and upgrades, so too are standard procedures evolving to identify opportunities for in-house improvements. These procedures are similar to activities performed in graduate schools and are aided by computer software that can perform statistical analyses of data. As the number of people with graduate degrees has increased and technology has grown, these continuous work-improvement procedures have become more common in the workplace.

The general procedures for making improvements involve collecting data or conducting a pre-implementation survey, analyzing the results, selecting the improvements to be made, developing and implementing an improvement plan, and conducting a post-implementation statistical analysis or survey to determine whether the plan worked.

Pre-implementation surveys are sent to important stakeholders such as division managers, program workers, customers, clients, or constituents. Surveys can also be sent to other governmental entities performing the same services. Software is readily available (and quite user-friendly) to collect data, conduct surveys, and analyze data and survey findings.

Pre-implementation surveys are usually exploratory surveys or measurement surveys; often both methods are used in one survey. An exploratory survey asks open-ended questions about what program components or services are causing problems or should be improved. The advantage of exploratory questions is that they allow the respondent to identify any number of issues and suggest program improvements with few restrictions. The disadvantage is that they do not allow for quantification or statistical analysis.

A measurement survey asks questions that can be quantified, such as "How well is Service A working on a scale of one to five?" The value of quantitative surveys is that findings can be measured and compared in terms of level of importance or need. This process allows for opportunities to be prioritized. Quantified findings can often be analyzed to determine whether certain problems are caused by a common, previously unrecognized factor. Quantified questions can also measure different levels of service between groups of staff or constituents in order to expose uneven, unfair, or discriminatory practices. A disadvantage of quantified analyses is that findings might not be statistically significant, i.e., better than a one-in-twenty probability of occurring from random chance. Even when the findings are statistically significant, they might not be great enough to warrant an improvement plan.

For broader applications, an explanatory survey can be conducted through an interview process. Such a survey is used to explain how a program operates, what parts of a program are working well, and what parts are working poorly. Findings on program activities that are working well can be used to develop best practices, and findings on activities that are working poorly can be used to identify industry-wide problems or challenges that have not previously been recognized or addressed. A disadvantage of explanatory surveys is that the process relies heavily on the abilities of the interviewer to ask probing questions, correctly analyze the information, and write lucid findings. The process can also be time-consuming and expensive.

Once the findings from the pre-implementation survey have been reported, staff develop an improvement plan. Many smaller improvements can be implemented with minimum impact on work production, work behaviors, or work systems, so making improvements is not necessarily restricted just to the people on special projects involved with systems conversions and upgrades. Still, improvement plans frequently involve some system changes and require the services of an in-house computer programmer, a bureau or division liaison, and a business systems analyst.

Post-implementation surveys and data analyses are used to determine whether improvement plans were correctly implemented and effective in addressing the recommendations. These findings can also identify unintended, negative effects from the plan.

Work Innovations

The stages for making innovations include the stages used for making improvements—design, create, test, implement, monitor, and correct—but innovations include an additional stage—invent. An innovation improves the lives of a significant portion of a population and will require major adjustments in work systems to accommodate the change. Perhaps the best example in recent years is the introduction of the desktop computer to the workplace. This innovation has generated numerous advantages to completing work. Processing personnel transactions electronically and communicating by way of e-mail quickly come to mind. At the same time, understanding and using computer software and hardware has required a major adjustment by workers.

Many recent innovations are derived from technology—bar codes, wireless communications, and the Internet, to name a few—but others are derived from a change in political or administrative direction. The Civil Rights Act was a political innovation insofar as it dramatically advanced legal protections against discrimination and led to innumerable organizational changes and adjustments in order to comply with new legal requirements. For more than a generation, the courts have been interpreting the meaning of the legislation in lawsuits between people seeking to enforce the requirements of the act and people seeking to protect once-legal privileges.

SELECTED LITERATURE REVIEW

The focus of this chapter's selected literature review is conflict management. Perhaps the greatest danger to an organization's work behavior is interpersonal conflicts and disputes. Morrill and Thomas (1992) describe conflict in an organizational setting as one stage in a three-stage process consisting of grievance, conflict, and disputing. Within this framework, they define grievance as a pre-conflict in which "a person or group reacts to a real or perceived violation of a set of norms, rules or individual or societal standards." Conflict is a progression into an "exchange of grievances . . . either directly or indirectly between individuals or groups" (404). Disputing, the third stage of the process, occurs when a third party is brought in and the situation becomes a public matter.

Conflict management style is the way individuals handle conflicts. Morrill and Thomas note that significant attention was given to conflict management style with the introduction of the book *The Managerial Grid* in 1964 by Blake and Mouton. "They argued that conflict management style could be measured along two managerial attitudes: concern for production and concern for people" (402).

These two attitudes parallel work production and work behaviors in the WPF. *The Managerial Grid* presents five conflict management styles: withdrawing (low concern for both production and people), smoothing (low concern for production and high concern for people), compromising (moderate concern for both production and people), forcing (high concern for production and low concern for people), and problem-solving or confronting (high concern for both people and production).

Morrill and Thomas developed the Disputing Process Instrument (DPI), which listed 15 behaviors covering the entire disputing process and grouped them into three dimensions—aggressiveness, authoritativeness, and observability. In the end, seven distinguishable styles emerged from their statistical analyses: avoidance, conciliatory negotiation, covert retaliation, discipline, overt retaliation, third-party mobilization, and toleration.

Hersey and Blanchard (1988) developed a theory of preferred, situation-based conflict management style according to the willingness and ability of staff to work. For example, they suggest a person who is unwilling and unable to work should be managed by concentrating on the worker's work production and giving limited attention to developing interpersonal relationships with her.

The reader who is interested in evaluating and improving conflict management in her workplace has a number of evaluative instruments available to use as pre- and post-implementation surveys that have been successfully tested in professional literature. Southworth (2000) notes that a prominent measurement of conflict management is the Thomas-Kilmann Conflict Mode Instrument (the Mode), which identifies five styles of conflict management (avoiding, accommodating, competing, compromising, and collaborating) predicated on two dimensions (assertiveness and cooperativeness).

Other conflict management-style instruments include the managerial grid, the Rahim Organizational Conflict Inventory II (ROCI II), the Organizational Communication Conflict Instrument (OCCI), and the Disputing Process Instrument (DPI).*

Another way to deal with conflict is conflict resolution. The distinction between conflict management and conflict resolution is that the first identifies a continuing process, whereas the second suggests an end or conclusion. Carnevale and Pruitt (1992) identify four primary procedures for resolving conflicts: struggle, negotiation, mediation, and arbitration. The goal of these procedures is to reach an agreement. As with certain conflict management models, some negotiating models use concern for self-interest and concern for others' interests as variables in the process.

Because circumstances can change, conflict resolution by negotiation, mediation, and arbitration generally is framed to encompass a specified period of time. For the HR manager, this is typically done in the negotiated labor agreement. Moreover, clauses in a labor contract can allow for certain elements of the agreement to be reopened or renegotiated while preserving continued agreement for the majority of the issues over the life of the contract.

---

* Studies on conflict management styles and instruments include Morrill and Thomas (1992), (DPI, managerial grid, OCCI, and ROCI II); Putnam and Wilson (1982), (OCCI); Thomas and Kilmann (1974), (the Mode); Hammock et al. (1990), (ROCI II); Chua and Gudykunst (1987), (OCCI); McFarland and Culp (1992), (OCCI); Witteman (1992), (OCCI); Mills et al. (1985), (the Mode); and Kirkbride et al. (1991), (the Mode).

People often accept promotions and assignments that lead to conflicts without proper preparation or the understanding of what difficulties may arise. On the other hand, some people decline a job or a promotion because they fear conflicts and do not want to deal with them. Still, there have been many training programs on managing conflicts. HR managers must be keenly aware of the impact of conflicts within the organization and provide programs that help staff to understand conflicts and how to deal with them.

HUMAN RESOURCE PROGRAMS TO MANAGE WORK PROCESSES

The HR manager develops and maintains the organizational chart and the classification plan to assist program managers. The organizational chart provides a concise layout of the organization in terms of its divisions, bureaus, sections, or units; the number and titles of the staff assigned to the various parts of the organization; and the hierarchy of the organization (i.e., who reports to whom). The classification plan contains the information on all the various classes of positions, including duties, salary grade, and qualifications.

The Organizational Chart

The structure of work processes is laid out in an organizational chart, which identifies the reporting structure of an organization. Generally, program managers of line operations report to officers who oversee a set of programs, and these officers, in turn, report work results and concerns to an executive officer, who reports to the agency head. Some functions, like the communications office, the strategic planning office, or the counsel's office, may be part of the executive team and report directly to the agency head.

The administrative operations, including the HR program, might report to the executive officer or directly to an agency head. Recently, there have been attempts inside the HR community to elevate the HR officer to the level of a strategic player who needs to be at the table with the chief executive officer (CEO), chief financial officer (CFO), and chief information officer (CIO).

The organizational chart for an operating unit is often presented in more detail to provide a fuller accounting of its functions. This chart might list specific positions and perhaps the names of the incumbents. This level of detail is mirrored in the organization's budget, which lists the expenses for general operations, specific functions, and fill levels.

The Classification Plan

In the public sector, equal pay for equal work is implemented through position classification. The HR staff assists the program managers in developing a description of duties, classifying a position under a new or existing title, allocating a salary or salary grade, and placing the position in a jurisdictional classification. A jurisdictional classification of "competitive" means the position must be filled through competitive examination in accordance with merit-system requirements. Positions placed in other jurisdictional classifications do not need to be filled by competitive examinations, and incumbents may not enjoy protections against at-will termination.

The classification plan includes duties descriptions for each position in the organization identified in the organizational chart. Duties descriptions list the general activities and important tasks for each title, and they may also list the knowledge, skills, and abilities (KSAs) or competencies required to perform the tasks and activities.

Job analysis links duties to critical job qualifications and competencies that are evaluated in employment tests as mandated by the courts. Decades ago, some selection and screening processes were used to systematically discriminate against minorities, particularly in the South. As a result courts have stated that a direct relationship must exist between the contents of the screening and selection process and the requirements to complete the work. This has led to *bona fide occupational qualifications* (BFOQs). Rather than focusing on optimal performance, BFOQs focus on minimum qualifications to do the job, with an eye on expanding opportunities for people to compete for these positions through competitive civil service examinations.

At the same time, the courts have been receptive to using *content validity* for defending the legality of civil service examinations. Rather than requiring HR agencies to correlate test scores with actual job performance (criterion validity), a technique that could be extremely expensive and time-consuming, the courts turned to content validity, which is based on closely reviewing and analyzing the duties of a class of positions and testing for the specific KSAs needed to complete the work. Thus the classification plan is an important resource for linking HR inputs to HR work processes, conducting civil service examinations, and defending recruitment, examination, and selection procedures.

KEY PERFORMANCE MEASURES

For HR managers, the key performance indicators for work processes involve position classification. Are there duties descriptions for all titles? Do the duties descriptions link KSAs or competencies to the required duties? Are positions being classified on a timely basis?

Table 5-1 presents a hypothetical situation involving six classification concerns: the existing inventory of classification documents, classification production, classification backlog, average classification-cycle times, denied or withdrawn requests, and classification-completion rates.

TABLE 5-1 Sample Classification Measures

	Positions Classified		
Classification Inventory	**All**	**w/ Duties Description**	**w/ KSA linkage**
Start of 2007	2450	2450	1875
End of 2007	2478	2478	1900
Change	28	28	25
Classification Production	**All**	**New Positions**	**Reclassifications**
Annual Average 2004–2006	165	85	80
2007	168	90	78
Change	3	5	–2
% Change	2%	6%	–3%
Production Targets	**167**	**88**	**79**
2007 vs. Target	1	2	–1
Backlog			
Start of 2007	50	25	25
End of 2007	48	24	24
Change	–2	–1	–1
Average Cycle Time (Business Days)			
Annual Average 2004–2006	64	80	46
2007	66	79	50
Change	2.0	–1	4
Percent Change	3%	–1%	9%
Target Cycle Times	**61**	**75**	**45**
2007 vs. Target	5	4.0	5.0
Denied/Withdrawn Requests			
Annual Average 2004–2006	28	18	10
2007	15	11	4
Change	–13	–7	–6
Percent Change	–46%	–39%	–60%
Completion Rate			
Annual Average 2004–2006	85%	83%	89%
2007	92%	89%	95%
Target Completion Rate	**93%**	**93%**	**93%**
2007 vs. Target	–1%	–4%	2%

The first section of Table 5-1 shows how many positions exist and how many of them have duties descriptions and linkages to KSAs. Since a duties description is generally required in order to classify a position, all positions are shown to have a duties description. However, more than 500 positions do not have KSAs linked to the duties. This linkage is necessary for the job analysis required to develop examinations according to professional standards. This information can also serve as an inventory of staff skills to determine whether the organization has sufficient HR capacity. If HR capacity is insufficient, this information can be used to develop recruitment and training plans to address capacity shortfalls.

The second area of Table 5-1 presents classification production. Overall the table shows that classification production was nearly the same for the annual average for 2004–06 and for 2007. The third section shows the backlog of classification requests. These figures show a slight reduction in classification requests that are not yet completed.

The fourth section of Table 5-1 shows average classification cycle times. The sample reveals that the average cycle time for new position classification requests fell slightly from an annual average of 80 business days during the baseline period of 2004–06 to 79 business days in 2007, but it increased for reclassification requests from 46 to 50 business days in 2007.

Next are the number of classifications that were denied or withdrawn. The last section of Table 5-1 shows the completion rates for classification requests, which is the number of completed requests divided by the total number of requests, including those completed and those withdrawn or denied. The completion rate increased slightly from 85 percent during the baseline period of 2004–06 to 92 percent in 2007, but it remains slightly below the target of 93 percent.

The information in Table 5-1 can be used to set or adjust future targets. If there is no reason to believe that productivity will increase, the target figures for the coming year should match the baseline figures from previous yearly averages. If targets are set for improved productivity, there should be an intervention or change in work production conditions. Interventions might include additional staff, new technology, process improvements, or additional training.

For example, in looking at the individual classification requests that were denied or withdrawn, the HR manager might find that the requests were not well prepared. An appropriate intervention might be to train agency staff on the most effective justifications for requesting a classification action. Or the HR manager might find that many of the requests had to be returned for revisions because they were missing important information. The HR manager might provide a checklist for staff on required information for classification requests.

With a data source to track changes in work production, the HR manager can determine whether the intervention worked. Moreover, through practice and reviewing other interventions, targets can be made more reliable. One of the complaints about performance targets is the lack of an improvement strategy or intervention to improve performance, so the implied way to reach the target is to let workers know they are being watched and must work harder. Ideally, computerized tracking systems should not be used heavy-handedly with staff, but to help the HR manager solve production problems.

THE FUTURE STATE OF HUMAN RESOURCE MANAGEMENT AND RESEARCH OPPORTUNITIES

Work production, work behaviors, and work improvements/innovations are separated into different work processes in the WPF. By doing this, the WPF is able to show how work processes involve more than just producing a service or a product. Appropriate work behaviors are needed to build strong relationships with employees and constituents, and guidelines on acceptable work behaviors are required to ensure that an organization is adequately protected against litigation from unfair or discriminatory practices.

Work improvements are no longer a surprise or an exception to the work experience, but rather an integral part of normal business operations. Many improvements to work processes have occurred in recent decades, mostly through advances in technology and the analysis of business processes. These improvements have produced more efficient and effective work procedures and have enabled a reduction in staffing levels, particularly of those workers performing routine procedures.

Interpersonal skills are recognized as requirements for leadership positions and working in a team environment. Business system analysis and computerization are key components of the new continuous-improvement work environment, so people need to understand the latest technology and how to use it to increase productivity.

Working within the WPF, researchers have the opportunity to explore how the work inputs of competencies, effort, and power fit with the work processes of work production, work behaviors, and work improvements. How does the value of the technology worker who improves work processes and achieves enormous gains in productivity compare to the value of the leader who advocates for the organization, builds its customer base, and attracts the necessary resources for conducting business? How does the value of the worker who provides the direct services compare with the value of the worker who provides the infrastructure support? How are competencies, effort, and power applied in these very different work processes? Where will there be abundant competencies and where will there be shortages? Is there a life cycle to work process improvements that will cause the rapid increase in work productivity to level off, or will there be even greater process improvements? How will these changes affect the future workforce and work environment? What will become of the average worker?

This chapter divides work processes into three distinct areas: work production, work behaviors, and work improvements. Classification activities are used to inventory existing jobs, categorize job titles, describe duties, and identify the required competencies. These activities are essential to align human resources with work functions, identify HR capacity shortages, and manage work performance. In Chapter 6, we discuss the outputs derived from these work processes: services, interpersonal communication, and improved services, processes, and systems.

CHAPTER 6

Work Outputs: The Direct Results of the Work

This chapter moves from the work processes described in Chapter 5 to the direct results of those processes—outputs—and to the need to measure efficiency in productivity and performance. The chapter first provides a selected literature review on the history of the productivity movement, followed by background information on outputs as presented in the Work Performance Framework (WPF). It then presents an inventory of HR services, identifies key performance measures for service efficiency, and looks at the future state of HR outputs and research opportunities. The chapter concludes with a second look at what makes a good worker.

SELECTED LITERATURE REVIEW

Before discussing work outputs, it is useful to review the history of the productivity movement in the public sector. Geert Bouckaert (1990) presents both chronological and methodological overviews of productivity movements in the public sector from approximately 1900 to 1990. Bouckaert described the first period, 1900–1940, as "government by the efficient."

While public-sector managers in the 19th century had been interested in eliminating the spoils system and corruption, by the turn of the century attention turned to making government efficient. Late in the 19th century, Frederick W. Taylor introduced "scientific management" to deal with the mechanistic aspects of efficiency and became a staunch publicist and advocate beginning in 1901. In 1900 Frank Johnson Goodnow asserted the need to separate administration from politics. Professionalism was equated to efficiency.

Bouckaert identified the next period, from 1940–1970, as "government by the administrator." Early in this period the focus shifted from scientific management to general management, with more attention given to the effectiveness of public programs. Political interests were recognized as an important factor in administering public programs, requiring public managers to be sensitive to the political issues addressed by public programs. By the end of this period, public administration as an academic discipline was divided into political science and administrative science, and attempts to measure effectiveness and tie these measures to costs led to techniques such as the planning programming budgeting system (PPBS), management by objectives (MBO), and zero-based budgeting (ZBB).

The next period, 1970–1980, Bouckaert called "government by the managers." Efficiency and effectiveness were both important, but the strongest motivation was to control government expenses that were seemingly out of control. Productivity concerns were based on "the desire to get more yield out of the taxpayer's money" (Bouckaert, 59). Important leaders of this period were "the political managers: governors, senators and mayors" who had to fund and manage public programs with fewer resources (Bouckaert, 59).

The final period, 1980–1990, Bouckaert called "government by the private sector." In the face of huge government deficits, officials sought to mimic the private sector by increasing productivity to produce savings and control expenses. At the same time, technological advances were beginning to occur, as computers began to be used to monitor and measure performance and systematically identify fraud, waste, and abuse.

One could argue that another period has occurred since 1990, which we might call "government by the innovators." Continuous improvements in public administration are now the norm. Today we believe not only that government should be effective and efficient but also that dramatic improvements are to be expected on a regular basis through the use of technology, and there will be a multiplying effect on the benefits of these advances.

The importance of the human factor in work and in social programs has been relegated to a somewhat lower position during the last three decades. Workers, particularly those with marginal skills that can be replaced by foreign labor, have witnessed their voices being silenced, and there has been growing inequality in wealth. The next trend in public programs will likely refocus on the human factor by redistributing some of the disproportionately accumulated wealth to the less wealthy and improving working conditions, both nationally and globally.

Bouckaert notes the existence of two very different economic views of government. The first is that government is primarily a *consumer* of goods and services. In this model, government consumes and produces equal amounts of resources. This zero-sum model holds that all funds taken from the economy by the government equal government outputs placed back into the economy, so it makes no difference to the condition of our economy whether government is very large or very small.

The second view is that government is primarily a *producer* of goods and services. Here, government productivity can vary and affect our gross national product and economy. The equation for government productivity (or efficiency) for this model is the ratio of outputs divided by inputs.

Over time, productivity concerns went beyond outputs to include the human factors involved with work outcomes, including job satisfaction and the effects of public programs on people and society. Although computers are capable of measuring large amounts of data, program managers continue to struggle to create meaningful measures of public program outcomes, so measuring outputs has remained a critical interest for measuring government performance. Bouchaert notes, however, that "national accounts still assume a mainly consuming government. This means that government production is measured by the consumption of resources needed for whatever government might produce" (69).

There are three important areas for evaluating productivity: efficiency, effectiveness, and rate of improvement. Efficiencies are tied to outputs, whereas effectiveness is more closely associated with outcomes and impacts. Rate of improvement attaches timeframes to gains in efficiency and effectiveness; whatever today's measures of efficiency and effectiveness might be, tomorrow's measures must be better, and the HR manager must continually look for ways to reach tomorrow's goals.

WORK OUTPUTS IN THE WORK PERFORMANCE FRAMEWORK

Work outputs are categorized according to the three work processes in the WPF. The outputs of public-sector work production are mainly services; the output of work behaviors is interpersonal communication; and the outputs of work improvements and innovations are new or improved systems and outputs. (See Figure 6-1, "Work Performance Framework—Work Outputs.")

FIGURE 6-1 Work Performance Framework—Work Outputs

Work Processes	Work Outputs	Efficiency Measures
Work Production	Services	*Cost per Unit of Output* *Intake* *Work Production* *Backlog* *Completion Rate* *Cycle Time* *Timeliness* *Accessibility*
Work Behaviors	Interpersonal Communication	*Behavior Problems* *Communication* *Problems*
Work Improvements and Innovations	New or Improved Systems and Outputs	*Rate of Change* *Costs per Unit of Change*

Work Production Outputs

According to the National Bureau of Labor Statistics, the two major industrial sectors in the United States are the goods-producing industries and the service-providing industries. Nationally, private-sector goods-producing industries account for one-sixth of all non-farm jobs, while private-sector service-providing industries account for about two-thirds of all non-farm jobs. Government services account for the final one-sixth of all non-farm jobs (U.S. Department of Labor 2008). Thus when we look at the outputs of work production in the government sector, we are generally talking about services.

To clarify the meaning of services, it is important to differentiate services from work behaviors. In the WPF the output of work behaviors is interpersonal communication, while the outputs of work production are services. Although positive work behaviors are important in carrying out services, work behaviors, per se, are not the service. For example, while a lawyer provides legal services, he must also adhere to work behavior standards to build trust and affiliation. His behaviors may be as important to his client's decision to use his services as the legal advice he provides, but his work behaviors are not the service.

Information is an important part of services. Service providers rely heavily on information as a resource and also provide information as a service. Because computers, the Internet, and telecommunications distribute and duplicate information almost instantaneously, work processes for using and sharing information have become more efficient and have led to improved services. To understand the role of information in services, it is helpful to see its uses. Related processes for providing services include:

- Providing forms, information, consultations, training, and reviews in support of the service

- Recording information on the service

- Notifying stakeholders of actions

- Tracking and analyzing data

- Identifying improvement opportunities

- Developing or revising laws, policies, or procedures

- Reporting on service activities and accomplishments.

When carrying out a service, information can be directly applied to completing work, such as when a doctor applies his knowledge to operating on a patient or when a computer programmer applies his knowledge to programming a computer system. Information can be used in an advisory capacity, such as when a mental health counselor suggests a treatment program to a patient by describing the benefits and risks of various options. Information can be explained, such as when a teacher explains sentence structure to a class of students. Or information can be shared, such as when a public service announcement informs people of the dangers of smoking cigarettes. As the related processes above show, information is documented through forms, databases, and reports.

As work has become more complex and professions require more specialized qualifications, greater knowledge of special professional or technical information is needed to perform the work. At the same time, as the categories of information become differentiated and computer systems evolve, delegation of services to dispense information has become more precise and efficient, and informational services have become tiered. For example, the medical specialist—a cardiologist, say, or an orthopedic surgeon—provides very specialized services; the general physician provides more general, lower-tiered services; and the physician's assistant handles routine cases. And the individual is able to treat himself by using resources such as online information, manuals that present information for self-diagnosis and treatment for minor problems, and pamphlets that present information for taking prescription and nonprescription drugs.

Organizations now look carefully at the level of complexity of the information needed for carrying out a service. For complex services at the highest tier, the expert provides the direct service by applying information that has been transformed into knowledge, skills, and abilities. In less complex situations, the responsibility moves from the service provider toward the recipient. Just below the top tier, the professional service provider advises the recipient on how to proceed, but the recipient applies his own judgment and makes the final decision. At the next lower tier, the service provider provides general information and explains certain intricacies about its applicability to a range of situations, in order for the customer to understand the options and select the one right for him. The lowest level is the least complex, where information is shared with the recipient, but the recipient is expected to interpret the information and draw his own conclusions on how to act.

Just as the invention of the printing press sped up the transfer of information, so too have the computer and the Internet. Moreover, personal digital assistants (PDAs) can hold vast amounts of data, so a person can access information anywhere, not just while sitting at a computer. Along with this increased availability of information are higher expectations that people will proactively use information as an enabling device in both their personal and professional lives. Because people have better access to the information they need, they have more control of their decision making, including being their own advisors and explainers of information.

These tiered services for sharing information now challenge how we look at training. While classroom training sessions might still be appropriate for providing some information, very often the information is used only occasionally and forgotten by the time it is actually needed. Under these circumstances, information needs to be provided on an as-needed basis. Thus Internet libraries are being created for people to get information on demand. Rather than giving all the information and possibilities, training for as-needed information explains what resources are available and lays out procedures to access the information on the Internet. Usually, a search engine is attached with the online information to help the user get to the right information quickly. The name of a contact person is also provided, in case the user needs help.

Work Behavior Outputs

The WPF presents interpersonal communication as the output of work behaviors; trust and affiliation (discussed as impacts in Chapter 8) are the effectiveness measures for interpersonal communication. While work behaviors and interpersonal communication are distinguished from work production processes and outputs, they are still relevant to work performance. Interpersonal communication presents information about who we are in terms of our values, emotions, attitudes, beliefs, and well-being.

Interpersonal communication can be regulated through impression regulation. Schlenker and Weigold (1992) note that impression regulation has been applied to a number of social phenomena, including helping behaviors, aggression, and anxiety. They identify three prominent motivators of impression regulation: self-glorification, self-consistency, and self-authentification. Self-glorification is the practice of maintaining and enhancing one's self-esteem, constructing one's "preferred" self, and compensating for weaknesses. Impression regulation for achieving self-consistency and self-authentification is when we present ourselves as we believe we are and reveal our personal identity.

Schlenker and Weigold note that self-identification should be believable and beneficial, but they acknowledge that people are capable of deception. Acquisitive impressions to gain favor reveal high self-esteem, personal control, and low anxiety, while protective impressions to avoid negative consequences reveal defensiveness, involving less social interaction and self-disclosure. Because the goals of self-glorification and self-revelation may conflict, we develop and present helpful interpersonal communications, and we monitor and avoid the unhelpful ones. Goffman expands impression regulation to seeing people as actors on a stage (Schlenker and Weigold 1992; Goffman 1959, 1971). We can probably think of someone who seems to always present himself by putting on a show.

According to Littlejohn (1992), interpersonal communication also transmits information about our group status based on three vectors: upward versus downward, positive versus negative, and forward versus backward. Littlejohn provides a table adapted from the works of Bales, Cohen, and Williamson (1979) depicting the characteristics associated with combinations of these vectors using three sets of symbols: U (upward) and D (downward); P (positive) and N (negative); and F (forward) and B (backward). For example, U is associated with "active, dominant, talkes a lot," while DNB is associated with "alienated, quits, withdraws" (304).

If we apply terms from the WPF, the symbols for positive and negative can be generally associated with work behaviors, i.e., the positive or negative personal interactions with others, while the symbols for forward and backward can be associated with work production, i.e., productive versus unproductive. The upward/downward vector addresses the concepts of dominance and submission, terms that are used sparingly in the WPF because of the recent movements toward flattening organizational hierarchies and work teams. While the goals of work behaviors as explained in the WPF are trust and affiliation, the goal of behaviors associated with dominance is power, including the power to distribute resources and opportunities.

One maxim of communication is that how one chooses to communicate depends upon the likely success of the communication strategy. A person might choose not to engage in interpersonal communication because he is unskilled or he believes he will expose weaknesses that will be counterproductive to his goals. He may also choose to limit interpersonal communication to the right situations, based on his level of comfort and expertise.

In the WPF, the benefit of interpersonal communication is building trust and developing affiliations. While deception is generally inappropriate, personal impressions need to be regulated to build trust and affiliation and avoid unnecessary revelations that might cause distrust or alienation. Interpersonal communication is a tool to motivate staff, build relationships within the organization and with customers, and develop networks that can lead to lateral and upward movement within or between organizations. Despite all these theoretical purposes and benefits of interpersonal communication, for many people interpersonal communication is its own reward. We simply enjoy communicating and being with people.

Work Improvement and Innovation Outputs

Since government is predominantly a service industry, outputs for governmental work improvements and innovations are mainly better services and systems.

Improved Services

Chapter 5 presented efficiency measurements for classification services. These measures related to taking inventory of existing classification documents and identifying the backlog of classification requests that still needed to be prepared. The chapter then looked at measuring classification production, average classification-cycle times, and classification completion rates.

Another measure of service efficiency is accessibility of the services, which is especially important as an efficiency measure for information because through computerization and the Internet, information can be made accessible instantaneously to a vast number of people all over the globe. Finally, average service costs provide perhaps the most important measure of efficiency because they provide the broadest means of comparison with other services and with comparable services in other organizations.

Improvements in interpersonal communication can be measured using the vectors of communication, with the goal to increase upward, positive, and forward communication. Interpersonal communication can also be measured by the increase in trust and affiliation of stakeholders. (These are effectiveness measures, which are discussed in Chapter 8.)

Improved Systems

While understanding, tracking, and measuring individual outputs are important in evaluating productivity gains, systems improved through advances in technology brought about the major benefits over the last two decades. These improvements generally involve an organization's computer infrastructure and infrastructure support. An example is the use of technology to electronically processes online tax documents, calculate refund amounts, and provide automatic tax refunds. These systems must be maintained and then updated when tax laws change and refunds become subject to a different set of calculations.

HUMAN RESOURCE PROGRAMS TO TRACK SERVICES

To achieve improvements, the HR manager must be able to record service activities, track data, and analyze service performance. The key HR service for this chapter is the HR information system, which serves two purposes. First, as a system for distributing information and performing calculations, the HR information system is a work-processing unit. Second, as the data source for performance measures, the HR information system helps to track work processes and outputs so the efficiency of HR programs and services can be monitored and improved.

Figure 6-2 lists HR strategic objectives that are tied to HR service objectives and HR services. This alignment helps the HR manager act strategically by using his services for building HR capacity, HR performance, and a strong work community.

FIGURE 6-2 Inventory of Human Resource Services

Human Resource Strategic Objective	Human Resource Service Objectives	Human Resource Services
Building Capacity	Staffing the Agency	Recruitment
		Examinations
		Position Classification
		Eligible List Maintenance
		Selection
		Retention
		Layoffs
	Staff Development	Traineeships
		Training and Development
Building Performance	Staff Performance	Performance Management
		Time and Attendance
		Personnel Assessment
		Probation Evaluation
		Performance Evaluation
		Human Resources Information System
	Diversity, Fairness, and Legal Compliance	Personnel Transactions
		Diversity
Building Community	Rewards and Benefits	Labor Relations
		Payroll Services
		Employee Benefits
		Workers' Compensation
		Employee Recognition
		Affirmative Action
	Work Environment	Organizational Health
		Employee Health and Well-Being

Activities must be identified for the various services, such as providing lists of candidates and processing appointments, conducting orientations for new workers, reviewing and recording probationary reports, reviewing and processing time and attendance sheets, and processing benefit claims.

The HR information system is where service information is recorded so that data on processing times and costs can be tracked and other variables can be identified and evaluated. When developing the information system, data specifications must be prepared to explain how the information will be used, what data fields are needed, and what efficiency measures will be tracked and analyzed. Data fields address the types of services, dates when the various stages of the process have been completed, and demographic information on the employee and his work location.

While HR managers must concentrate on the key performance measures that their officers are most interested in, they also need to track the performance of all services and activities at the operational level, always looking for opportunities to improve services and reduce costs.

KEY PERFORMANCE MEASURES

Figure 6-1 presents efficiency measures for HR services, including cost per unit of output, intake, work production, backlog, completion rate, cycle time, timeliness, and accessibility. Efficiency measures for interpersonal communication might include the number of behavioral and communication problems, with attention to specific employees and work locations within the organization. Efficiency measures for improvements and innovations include the rate of change in service efficiency and effectiveness, and the cost per unit of change.

Efficiency measures are needed to evaluate work production as well as work improvements and innovations. But where standardization is important in evaluating work production efficiency, change is important in evaluating the efficiency of improvements and innovations, and there is always a danger that change will have negative, unintended effects on service quality standards.

Data

When constructing the HR information system, the HR manager, referring to the inventory of HR activities in Figure 6-3, must address the following questions:

1. What are the important services to report?

2. Will the HR information system provide the following information?

    Intake: Number of requests for services

    Completed Services: Number of services completed; number of customers served

    Uncompleted Services: Number of services initiated but not completed (Does not include services still in process)

    Backlog: Services still in progress

    Completion Time: Business days from date service was requested to completion date

    Deadline: Time/date service is due to be completed (e.g., payroll services have a one-pay-period fixed deadline)

    On time services: Number of services completed by deadline

    Late services: Number of services not completed by deadline

3. Will we be able to track the following efficiency measures for our important services?

    Work Production: Number of completed services; number of customers served

    Completion Rate: $\dfrac{\text{Number of completed services}}{\text{Number of completed and uncompleted services}}$

    Backlog: Number of service requests still in progress

    Average Cycle Time: Average completion time

    Timeliness (Rate of on-time services): $\dfrac{\text{Number of on-time services}}{\text{Number of on-time and late services}}$

Baseline measures: Average efficiency measures for preceding time period

Targets: Projected higher efficiency measures based on an improvement plan

4. Will we be able to track HR staff time?

    Who is working on what activities?

    How much time is the staff working on each activity or its subparts?

Baseline measures are the average times of past performance that are used to predict future performance. Targets are projected performance estimates that are expected to be better than baseline measures. However, the HR manager must keep in mind that there must be an intervention to set new standards. When an HR manager is setting a target for future performance, he must explain what will be done differently as the basis for expecting a different result. Tracking staff time on HR activities is critical in order to hold staff accountable for their work performance, set individual performance goals, and track costs.

Transaction Cost

Once the services have been identified and the HR information system has been set up, the HR manager must identify the unit of measure. The unit of measure for service costs is the transaction. This efficiency measure is derived by dividing outputs by inputs. The transaction consists of providing a service and receiving payment for that service. Total HR service production includes all HR transactions completed for an organization.

The work production system has three parts: service activities, administration, and infrastructure support. To measure the average transaction cost, it is necessary to add indirect service costs and the costs for capital and equipment to the transaction costs in addition to direct service costs. To facilitate the process of measuring transaction costs, these ancillary costs can often be aggregated. For example, administrative HR costs might add 15 percent to the cost of each individual transaction, and the infrastructure cost, including capital and equipment, might add an additional 20 percent. In this case, the average transaction cost includes the direct service cost and a 35 percent adjustment cost for administration and infrastructure support.

Because transactions can be as brief as a telephone call or as long as producing a report that involved hundreds of person-days of work, different transactions have different costs. When the transactions are very small and frequent, the unit of measure can be aggregated to workload time on transactions. So, for example, the unit of measure for answering phone calls can be described as "15 percent of time involves answering phone calls." Actual telephone time can be confirmed by telephone usage reports. Ancillary work activities can also be aggregated. For example, staff on-the-job training could be described as "10 percent of time involves on-the-job training of staff." Staff costs can be prorated for time spent on these special services to determine transaction costs.

Many transactions are computerized, so computerized transaction costs must include costs for infrastructure support to maintain and upgrade the computer system. Because computers have reduced transaction processing time, the number of people processing transactions has become a smaller proportion of transaction costs, while the number of people maintaining and upgrading computer systems that process transactions has become larger. Information on aggregated costs as well as transaction costs is useful when comparing similar work activities, similar work outputs, or similar organizations. These costs are also useful when measuring the change in efficiency following systems conversions and upgrades.

Cycle Time

The unit of measure for service processing time is the cycle time. There are distribution costs associated with providing services as well as costs to the recipient to access the services. The access cost includes time spent by the customer, so the faster and more convenient the access, the less expensive the transaction is for the customer. One of the benefits of making a distinction between services and information is that sharing of information can be computerized. Using a website, an organization can make its information available to the public, so accessibility can change from one customer speaking to one worker to anyone with a computer having instant access to information posted on the Internet. Still, the time to navigate the Internet can be lengthy, so a customer might believe he is losing valuable time, even though he is able to access the service or information on his computer.

Cycle times are valuable information because they can be broken down into subparts. For example, providing a list of candidates to an operating division to fill a position might involve posting an announcement for the vacancy, reviewing resumes, canvassing an eligible list, and preparing the list. By tracking the results of postings, one might find that a certain time of the year is most effective for getting the information out to potential applicants and meeting the need of the division to get the list quickly.

While these discussions have been somewhat detailed, the important overall point is that HR managers need to track their performance in order to evaluate program efficiency, design interventions, and set credible targets.

THE FUTURE STATE OF HUMAN RESOURCE MANAGEMENT AND RESEARCH OPPORTUNITIES

The public-sector HR community has begun to realize that it needs to have a better understanding of operational performance. The first step is to understand HR outputs as services and how to measure these outputs. Whether by intention or disinterest on the part of HR managers, there is a shortage of available data on the costs and cycle times of HR services. Moreover, there is little data available on what activities are being performed and how the HR staff is involved in these activities.

There is a growing interest in the HR community in understanding and establishing benchmarks for HR services, but these efforts are generally thwarted by this lack of understanding of service efficiency and how to measure it. If HR managers are serious about being strategic partners in the upper levels of organizational management, they must actively pursue better methods of measuring the efficiency of their services.

While the HR research community has provided extensive data analyses and case studies on HR outcomes, it has paid much less attention to the operational level of understanding, measuring, and analyzing service efficiency. Moreover, because of the lack of a unifying theoretical framework, there has not been a clear presentation of how the various segments of research can address the broader needs of the HR manager. The WPF can serve as this guide. Still, the HR research community must become more involved with understanding and tracking HR service efficiency.

WHAT MAKES A GOOD WORKER?

Previously, we looked at what makes a good worker from the perspective of the antecedents to work performance—i.e., as a human resource and as participants in enabling opportunities. Now we revisit the question from the perspective of work inputs, processes, and outputs.

From the vantage point of inputs, the good worker is someone who applies the needed competencies to his work. These competencies include professional and technical talents, administrative and managerial skills, and behavioral KSAs. The good worker is also someone who demonstrates high effort by looking beyond the work that comes into his in-basket, setting goals to expand his work activities into new areas with higher performance targets, and persevering in the face of adversities and work challenges.

The good worker also understands the role of power and seeks the authority to act, uses resources appropriately, influences others by making sound decisions, communicates information effectively, and uses interpersonal skills to gain cooperation and support.

At the work process level, the good worker is productive. He understands and uses administrative and infrastructure resources effectively; he understands and uses appropriate work behaviors in order to develop trust and affiliation; and he understands and uses the tools for continuous improvement to increase his own productivity and the productivity of his organization. At the output level, the good worker provides efficient direct or indirect services, communicates his work and his aspirations to others, listens to and understands their interests and concerns, and helps to build better work systems and services.

While the good worker may not be strong in every ability, activity, or output, he must perform his role well and understand the roles of the other members of his organization. He must understand the other work processes and how they contribute to completing the work of the organization. He must understand the various outputs and how they are evaluated. Finally, he must understand how his work and the work of others can be improved to build HR performance.

Work outputs have been somewhat overlooked recently as strategic planners have focused on program outcomes, and more specifically program benefits. However, any claims to high productivity can be confirmed only by documenting the important transactions completed by the HR provider, measuring the cost per transaction, and comparing transaction costs to those of comparable organizations. Moreover, in today's environment of continuous improvement, any claims about increased productivity can be confirmed only by comparing the transaction costs prior to improvement initiatives to the transaction costs following implementation.

Efficiency, while not the only measure of work performance, is an essential part of it.

Efficiency measures cannot always assure managers that their workers are highly productive. Still, they are critical for reporting and managing performance. Chapters 7 and 8 will address the second part of productivity—effectiveness—by looking at program outcomes and impacts.

PART 3

Outcomes and Impacts: The Real and Perceived Consequences of Work

Outcomes

T his chapter begins with background information on outcomes in
the context of the Work Performance Framework (WPF). It continues with a general look at HR programs that address outcomes,
leading to a discussion of key performance measures for assessing
worker and HR program performance. It then looks at the future state of
HR management and research opportunities on issues related to HR program outcomes. The chapter does not include a selected literature review,
but many references are cited in the background information,

The WPF has three sets of outcomes: program outcomes, HR outcomes, and evaluation outcomes. (See Figure 7-1.)

FIGURE 7-1 Work Performance Framework—Outcomes

Program Outcomes
Program Benefits
Solving and Preventing Social Problems
Providing Care
Enabling People
Advancing Social Justice
Unintended Consequences
Decreased Benefits

Human Resource Outcomes
Rewards
Response to Success
Punishments
Response to Failure
Response to Violations
Obligations
More Difficult, Complex Work
Adversities
Dangers
Time Constraints
Conflicts
Evaluation Outcomes
Performance Measurements
Worker Performance
HR Program Performance
Assessments of Fairness
Equity
Equality
Due Process, Right to Dissent
Social Contract

PROGRAM OUTCOMES

While most attention on program outcomes is given to benefits, unintended consequences are program outcomes that can negate the benefits. Part of an effective program is avoiding undesirable, unintended consequences to the fullest extent possible.

Generally, public-sector program managers are more attuned to the effectiveness of their programs than to the efficiency of their programs. Very often, their focus on effectiveness is more attuned to avoiding risks and unintended consequences that might bring unwanted attention to their programs than it is to facilitating prominent program successes. One reason for this line of thinking is that public-sector program managers operate in a more stable environment than the private sector, so they tend to be protective of their staff and programs.

Program Benefits

The WPF posits two fundamental purposes of public programs: (1) Public programs must provide *important services* that should not or cannot be provided by private businesses, and (2) government is responsible for advancing *social justice.* The WPF further proposes that the purposes of public program services are to solve or prevent societal problems; provide care and compassion; and, through the distribution of information and other resources, enable people to solve their own problems.

Social justice components include (1) equitable laws and procedures that create a level playing field on which people who are motivated to do their best can enjoy substantial individual rewards; (2) distribution or redistribution of the nation's wealth and resources, especially to the neediest citizens; (3) due process and freedom of speech as mechanisms for citizen dissent; and (4) the social contract that holds people accountable for being responsible citizens and for helping themselves to the fullest extent possible, particularly when aided by public programs.

Program benefits are often difficult to explain when the purpose is to prevent problems from occurring. While tracking crime is relatively straightforward, reducing crime may be very expensive and difficult to achieve. Preventing disasters such as a nuclear melt-down can be very expensive without discernible proof that less protection could have accomplished the same level of prevention. On the other hand, Hurricane Katrina revealed that cutting back on the disaster prevention activities of maintaining levees can appear to be inconsequential until the critical moment when disaster strikes.

Enabling programs are also difficult to evaluate because their success depends on the recipient's using the public program effectively. For example, did the program recipient who received training actually get a job? Many public administrators now focus on outcomes of enabling programs (e.g., subsequent employment) more carefully than on outputs (e.g., number of training classes completed, number of people receiving training). Often, enabling programs yield successful outcomes for only the more promising recipients, which causes the dilemma of how to address service recipients whose prospects for completing the training or finding subsequent employment are extremely low.

In the present environment, sustaining existing levels of services is insufficient to meet citizen expectations. We expect continuous improvements. When we buy a car, we anticipate there will be changes that make the new car better than the one we had before, such as a remote entry system, improved energy efficiency, and computerized monitoring systems. The same is true with government services; people expect improvements. This can create even greater misgivings about programs that must show positive outcomes while working with the most difficult cases.

An example of noticeable service improvements in a public agency is the local offices of the New York State Department of Motor Vehicles (DMV). In the past there were long waiting lines with abrupt clerks who might explain to the disgruntled customer who had waited in line for 30 minutes that she was missing information or documents. The customer might then need to go to the end of the line or to her insurance agent's office to gather the missing material and come back another time. The entire experience was frustrating.

Now, many of the transactions can be completed by mail or over the Internet, without the need to even visit the DMV. When a trip is necessary, the first stop is the information desk, where all the papers are checked to see that they are in order before the customer finds herself waiting. Moreover, the customer can now sit down as she waits rather than stand in a line. The reduced waiting time is estimated for the customer, and a television or news bulletin gives the customer something to watch while passing the time. The clerk, who is now called a representative, is trained in providing courteous service, and her actions are closely monitored. The difference is like night and day.

Like most public-sector program managers, the HR manager seeks program successes. The WPF identifies three strategic objectives or planned benefits for HR program: building HR capacity, building performance, and building community. By focusing on these strategic objectives, the HR manager can align her HR programs with these objectives, seek to increase the effectiveness and efficiency of the HR programs, and thereby achieve these objectives.

Program Unintended Consequences

Changes do not necessarily bring about improvements; they can also make matters worse. Even when a change is properly implemented, unintended negative consequences can result. Public administrators are placed in a precarious position where improvements are expected but negative consequences will be closely scrutinized. While organizational leaders might claim they are looking for aggressive risk takers, they want successes, not failures. While failure might be tolerated for a while in some work environments, there are limits. What a leader is really seeking is a risk manager—a person who understands risks, limits vulnerabilities, and exploits opportunities. Two theories that address uncertain consequences are *expected utility theory* and *prospect theory*.

Expected utility is a decision-making theory based on outcomes and probability of success. This can be represented in the formula:

$$Outcome = Benefit \times Probability\ of\ Success$$

This concept is useful for actuaries where there is a great deal of data to predict mortality rates based on variables such as age, gender, and tobacco use. In many situations, however, the probability of an outcome is unknown.

Levy (1992) explains that "prospect theory has emerged as a leading alternative to expected utility as a theory of decision under risk" (171). He summarizes prospect theory as differing from expected utility because of the addition of a point of reference used to frame decisions. Referring to the works of Kahneman and Tversky (1979), he presents five general findings about decisions with uncertain outcomes:

1. "People tend to think in terms of gains and losses rather than changes in their net asset levels" (174).

2. "Losses loom larger than gains" (175).

3. "Individuals tend to be risk-averse with respect to gains, and risk-acceptant to losses" (174).

4. People tend to respond differently based on whether a dilemma is presented as a gain or a loss (177).

5. People tend to misapprehend probabilities (178).

Herbert and Katsulas (1992) discuss risk analysis and how it can be abused in policy debates because people misapprehend risk. They begin with a formula that focuses on losses by defining risk rather than outcome:

$$Risk = Probability \times Impact$$

The term "impact" here means a negative outcome. (Impacts in the WPF are presented as individual reactions to programs, outputs, or outcomes.)

Herbert and Katsulas argue that risk analysis in public-policy debates artificially assigns probability to arguments and overvalues arguments with potentially large losses. They cite other errors of risk analysis, including the fallacy of the golden mean, where implausibly high-loss estimates are averaged with conservative estimates, yielding an artificially high average, and the zero-infinity problem (Ehrlich and Ehrlich 1991), where, using the penultimate risk such as a nuclear war, "the skilled advocate can

effectively moot the importance of probability" (9). Among their suggestions for improving risk analysis are (1) acknowledge that some risks are
so trivial that they are not meaningful; (2) evaluate the risk and not an
incremental increase (e.g., doubling a one-billion-to-one risk); and (3) do
not become enslaved to large impacts without regard to relative risk.

Risk analysis is especially confounding because there are dangers today
that never existed before such as nuclear destruction, overpopulation,
and environmental degradation. The point is not that these risks should
be ignored, but that they need to be better understood. Solutions to address these risks must not be radicalized, but rather clarified. In general,
risk theory and prospect theory address the probability of specific positive or negative outcomes. They do not directly address the concept of
unintended consequences where these consequences are unknown or
unanticipated.

By presenting three strategic objectives for the HR manager—building
capacity, performance, and community—we can anticipate that if we
pursue one goal but not the other two, there might be unintended negative consequences. For example, an organization that is driven by performance but overlooks community-building activities risks losing capacity
due to retention problems. All three objectives must be addressed in a
comprehensive HR strategic plan.

HUMAN RESOURCE OUTCOMES

Rewards and punishments are the organization's response to the employee's work contribution, often accompanied by new or different obligations and adversities. Obligations include the increased workload and
work complexity of new assignments or the greater responsibility given in
conjunction with rewards. Adversities are similar to obligations, but they
involve dangers, conflicts, and time constraints that can create stress.

Rewards

Rewards and punishments are outcomes in the WPF because they are part of the service transaction. When public programs provide satisfactory services, their employees are rewarded; when the programs provide unsatisfactory services, their employees are punished. Unfortunately, because program benefits and unintended consequences have not always been shared with the public, the relationship between program benefits and individual rewards has not always been evident. Thus public program managers have been directed to measure program performance, become more transparent in setting goals and documenting achievements, and be more accountable for their successes and failures.

Organizations have begun to use employee-satisfaction surveys to gauge the effectiveness of their rewards and benefits, to retain workers and build strong organizational citizens. Intrinsic rewards often influence retention more than extrinsic rewards, particularly when jobs are plentiful and employees have viable options to seek employment elsewhere.

Extrinsic Rewards

Extrinsic rewards include:

- Salary
- Health insurance
- Retirement benefits
- Workers' compensation insurance
- Tenure protection
- Education and training programs
- Promotions and advancements.

Public service has a reputation for providing lower salaries than the private sector but better job protection and benefits. While there have been substantial gains over the last several decades, public-sector salaries and benefits vary from state to state and location to location. In New York, for example, state government jobs are viewed favorably in Albany, the state capitol, and in the more remote upstate locations where economic growth has lagged in recent times. In the New York City area, however, salaries are less attractive because of the higher cost of living. While there are geographic pay differentials or adjustments in certain areas of the state, they do not fully compensate for cost-of-living differences.

Tenure protection, while excellent for lower-level jobs, is more problematic for top jobs filled by political appointments. On the other hand, a person can receive a political appointment without going through the process of incremental promotions based on competitive civil service examinations.

Promotions are perhaps the most important method for retaining high-performing staff. Most often, promotions in New York state government are made by using competitive examinations in accordance with the state's constitution. However, as noted earlier, the validity of civil service examinations is somewhat low, leading to problems discussed later in this chapter.

Intrinsic Rewards

Intrinsic rewards include:

- Job-person fit
- Prestige
- Good worker relationships
- A good work environment.

Job-person fit is an intrinsic reward in which the worker enjoys her work because the job requirements match her talents and interests, while prestige refers to the importance a worker is given because of her job duties, special talents, competencies, role, or authority accorded by the organization. A good work environment can help create an enjoyable work experience, and good worker relationships help to build trust and affiliation between workers.

Employee recognition programs, mentoring/coaching programs, and work teams help to build good work relations and a friendly work environment. There have also been recent findings that having a best friend at work increases the intrinsic enjoyment of work. Job sharing, part-time work schedules, and telecommuting are programs that allow workers to adjust their work schedules to their special needs, which often include child or elder care.

Intrinsic rewards, which can be less costly for the organization than extrinsic rewards, can help to build worker loyalty and increase retention rates. A worker who has attained a salary that satisfies her needs may be more willing to forgo further salary increases in favor of improving her overall quality of life. It is often argued that intrinsic rewards can be more important than extrinsic rewards to attract and retain good workers. Intrinsic rewards are critical to building a strong work community.

Punishments

In today's work environment, the term *punishment* is avoided, if possible. A more positive approach is to identify what are called performance or developmental improvement opportunities. This language is important because we want workers to accept constructive feedback on their performance shortcomings. We also want to build a work community, and heavy-handed actions to address performance shortcomings can be harmful to that cause. The following discussion of punishments addresses the small number of cases where a worker's performance problems are significant, and where she conveys an underlying message of distrust and unwillingness that requires the organization to act forcefully. This does not necessarily mean that trust-building efforts should cease, however.

Punishments are meted out for incompetence, i.e., the person lacks the capability or competencies to perform required duties or produce work, and misconduct, i.e., she failed to follow appropriate work rules or behaviors. However, work violations can be more complex than these simple distinctions suggest. Power and effort were presented in Chapter 4 as other forms of HR inputs, and making a distinction between incompetence and misconduct in terms of effort and use of power can be very difficult. Was a certain action misconduct because the person applied very little effort, or was it incompetence because she does not have the physical stamina to persevere through a difficult assignment? Was the action due to misconduct because the person abused her power, or was the action due to incompetence because she did not know how to use her power correctly?

Misconduct includes carrying out illegal activities such as theft, improper use of public assets, sexual harassment, discrimination, violence, and use of illegal drugs. Often, employees will take a cue from their organization on whether improper activities are tolerated. If a person observes high-level officials acting improperly or tolerating illicit activities, she will probably be more inclined to participate in an illicit activity.

The unlawful employment of illegal immigrants is perhaps the most visible example of organizations condoning an illegal activity, although this is more common in the private sector than the public sector. Yet, some people believe certain laws and enforcement activities are unfair. While there may well come a time when laws on immigration and performance-enhancing drugs will be changed, the toleration of controversial illicit activities can bolster other illicit activities in the workplace.

Misconduct also includes less extreme forms of work behavior problems, such as conflicts with supervisors or staff, disrespectful actions, and intentional low effort. When a worker perceives she is being treated unfairly, she may be prone to sabotage her own work performance or the performance of others. A supervisor may be reluctant to confront a poor performer for fear of retaliation or even lower work performance. Nonetheless, punishment is an important management tool that must be fair, and the link between punishments and poor performance must be clearly explained and displayed.

Types of Punishments

Once a public worker is granted tenure following the completion of a probationary period, she becomes a permanent employee. In most cases, she is protected from termination without "cause," as legally defined, unless she serves at the pleasure of the appointing officer or a layoff occurs. Once cause is established, a punishment can be set by law (penalty) or negotiated between an agency and an employee.

Types of punishment include reprimand, fines, suspension without pay, demotion in grade and title, or dismissal from the service. When a worker is going to be terminated for cause, she will often be allowed to resign to avoid having a dismissal on her employment record.

Disciplinary Process

An agency can exercise its greatest discretion to terminate an employee while she is serving her probationary period, although even during probation she must be apprised periodically of how well she is performing. Once an employee is granted tenure, the disciplinary process is detailed by law or negotiated labor agreements. Because this process can be costly and protracted, it is important that an agency makes the best use of the probationary evaluation.

Generally, a punishment can be grieved, and the grievance process, including the right to representation by a union representative or counsel, is outlined in the labor contract. Whether a supervisor is evaluating an employee's performance during probation or as a part of a permanent employee's annual evaluation, performance problems should be well documented without speculating on one's motives.

Obligations and Adversities

While it may seem that rewards are the prize for good work, they usually come with some strings attached. When a person is rewarded with a promotion, she is simultaneously given new obligations, and she might also have more adversities to address.

Punishments are also accompanied by obligations; a person who is being punished is obliged to make corrective changes to her work performance or behaviors. Very often, even though a person might not actually be demoted, she might be punished by having certain work responsibilities taken away from her because her superior has lost confidence in her abilities or reliability.

While she might be taking a step backward by losing a growth and development opportunity that would enable her to be promoted or given more responsibility in the future, this situation often gives the appearance of rewarding poor performance with a lighter workload. When an organization has many workers who are given light work assignments because they do not perform well, the good workers often feel they are the ones being punished. This workload imbalance might be tolerated for a while, but over time the good workers will become dissatisfied with accommodating "free riders."

Obligations

New obligations that accompany an advancement or promotion include additional work, more difficult work, and supervisory or managerial responsibilities. The obligations can be applied to the three work processes identified in Chapter 5: work production, work behaviors, and work improvements.

Work production obligations might include taking on additional or more difficult services, overseeing the work production of other people, or taking on administrative duties such as personnel, budgeting, or reporting activities. Work behavior obligations might require increased activities in fostering customer relations or networking with people inside and outside the organization. Work improvement obligations might also involve taking on special assignments or projects. As a person is promoted into higher levels of the organization, she must be more cautious about using inflammatory language or burning bridges.

Adversities

Adversities often parallel obligations. Whereas obligations involve additional or more complex work activities, adversities can lead to increased stress or discomfort. The WPF presents three categories of stressors: (1) dangers, (2) time constraints, and (3) conflicts. While a person might feel she is entitled to a promotion and is willing to perform more difficult or complex work, she might be unwilling or unprepared to handle the adversities that come with an appointment or promotion. While steps can be taken to reduce stress in the workplace, some stressors might be unavoidable.

Dangers stem from uncertainty and high potential loss. While risks involving unintended negative consequences are coupled with program benefits, risks are also linked to appointments and promotions. Safety and health risks are most often associated with the protective and health care services, and from accidents involving tools and equipment.

Legal risks, which are mostly organizational risks, are often substantial in the public service, and are becoming even greater because of increased transparency. With the passing of the Freedom of Information Act, opportunities to access federal records have dramatically increased in recent years, and similar laws have been passed by various states providing access to their records. Programs, policies, procedures, and interpretations developed by an agency to carry out its programs can be questioned and challenged by program recipients and the general public. Because of this environment of high legal risk, correspondence and general communications are closely reviewed and monitored at every level of an organization.

For the individual worker, financial risks are generally associated with the entrepreneurial risks of starting and running a business. Most public programs that involve individual financial risks require the person to be bonded as a protection against financial losses, generally due to theft of assets. Most often in the public service, individual financial risk is associated with job loss, so the most vulnerable workers are those who serve at the discretion of the appointing officer. To offset these risks, people often establish back-up strategies, including associations with educational institutions or "think tanks."

The greatest risk of financial loss for the tenured career civil servant is the loss of a job from down-sizing or restructuring. Still, if someone loses her job as a result of the abolition or reduction of positions, she will often be placed on a preferred list and certified to fill the next job opening for that title. Nonetheless, she might be out of work for several months or even years, and in some cases never rehired if she served in a unique job title or location.

Reputation risks are very important in public service. While an elected official is not easily removed from office, she is vulnerable at the next election. Unelected officials who serve at the pleasure of the elected official are vulnerable to extremely swift action. A bad mistake can cost an organization's leader her job in an instant, and can cost her special appointees their jobs as well.

A reputation is built from the very beginning of one's career. Generally, those who are promoted to the highest positions have built strong reputations over a period of decades and were promoted early and often. In stark contrast, a person who has not been promoted may be resentful and act to sabotage the reputations of others. It is not unusual for a person's first supervisory assignment to involve overseeing the work of an employee whose reputation is poor and whose intentions are in doubt. The success she has in this early supervisory situation may affect her reputation and work opportunities for years to come.

While the WPF presents added duties as obligations, the problem of time constraints due to more work is an adversity and another source of stress. Much attention has been given to developing time-management strategies. For example, a person might set aside time at the beginning or end of the workday to work on correspondence or a special project. As duties accumulate, a person becomes more reliant on delegating work and holding her staff responsible for completing the work. Technology has become a critical tool for managing work time by organizing work, scheduling activities, and being accessible while doing other work.

Conflicts are also adversities. Chapter 5 discussed personality conflicts, and other conflicts involve demands of work and home, and ethics. Conflicts between demands from work and home can be a great source of stress. Although workers in the public sector generally have liberal amounts of vacation days, personal days, and sick days, a higher workload from a promotion might make taking time off more difficult. Childcare or elder care responsibilities can take an enormous amount of time and effort, and the stress over concerns for the child or parent can multiply the stress from work. Maintaining a strong relationship with a spouse and family members can be particularly difficult when a large project is due to be completed and overtime work is required.

Ethical conflicts that arise while enforcing legal provisions and still meeting political, social, customer, and staff needs and concerns can be highly stressful. Some constituents might demand special treatment or resources. Because political philosophies differ, a new administration might drastically change the way some programs are carried out, and the budgets of some programs might be cut in favor of new programs.

Often, the person who is promoted is the one who best handles adversities. While this fact is broadly recognized, it is readily shared in the organization. Lower-level staff often resent the higher pay and perquisites of higher-level staff in the organization, but fail to acknowledge the adversities they must also endure. Lower-level staff often overlook their own unwillingness to handle adversities, and sometimes their role in creating adversities.

EVALUATION OUTCOMES

Evaluation outcomes include performance measurement and assessments of fairness. Performance measurements provide information that explains successes and failures, and it used to allocate resources and to justify rewards and punishments. Fairness considerations determine whether services are equitable to the various customers and whether the rewards and punishments are equitable to staff.

Performance measurements are presented as outcomes in the WPF because managers must know how well their employees are performing and how well their programs are serving their intended purposes. Fairness is presented as an outcome because there are many parties interested in public programs, and providing special services for one group of constituents may be perceived as unfair to another group. Fairness is also an important issue to workers, not just to constituents and customers.

Performance Measurements

Performance measurement is an outcome in the WPF because it provides information that can be used to evaluate and link program and worker performance. There has been a great deal of attention given to performance measurement in recent years. The Balanced Scorecard, developed and introduced by Robert S. Kaplan and David P. Norton in 1993, aligns an organization's vision and strategies with four areas of performance: (1) learning and growth, 2) business processes, (3) the customer, and (4) financial performance.

This management technique also addresses both outputs and outcomes. Within the public sector, financial performance has likely been underemphasized, while the additional perspective of social justice is extremely important, demonstrating key differences between business administration and public administration. Still, there has been a move in recent years toward making public programs more efficient and "business-like."

Program performance is measured in terms of the efficiency of work processes to generate outputs, the effectiveness of the program outcomes, and the impact of the program on customers and stakeholders.

While an agency head is interested in measuring the program performance of her entire organization, the HR manager must specifically address her HR programs. Chapter 6 discussed inventorying the various HR programs and services and developing efficiency measures for services, costs, and cycle times. HR program effectiveness is measured by evaluating the degree to which the organization is building HR capacity, performance, and community through HR programs and services.

Rewards and punishments were presented above as worker outcomes, but they must be based on worker performance to be credible. In 1883 the Pendleton Civil Service Reform Act was passed as a response to President James Garfield's assassination by a disappointed office seeker, marking the beginning of the merit system for filling most federal jobs, and over time states followed by enacting parallel legislation of their own. All qualified people in the general public were thus able to compete for these positions by taking civil service examinations.

The use of civil service examinations has been questioned, however, because of their relatively low validity, generally in the range of .21 to .35. These validity coefficients mean that the rankings on the eligible lists accounted for between only 4 percent and 12 percent of the variation in worker job performance. Because these examinations cannot be relied on to place the best workers at the top of the eligible list, an agency is often placed in the dilemma of (1) filling a position with someone other than the best candidate; (2) creating a special position or seeking to have the position exempted from examination to avoid using the eligible list; or (3) requesting declinations from higher-standing candidates to reach the desired person.

While civil service law prohibits requiring a candidate to decline a promotion, there is no penalty for asking. Often, there are suggestions that a declination would put a person in a favorable light at some future time, but a definitive quid pro quo would be unlawful, so managers are very careful about how they state their declination requests. These strategies, while generally effective, often create the appearance that decisions are made based on special treatment or political interests.

The relatively low validity of civil service examinations can be attributed, in part, to the fact that they measure competencies required to perform the work but not actual work performance. Accurately assessing work performance is perhaps the most important task in all of HR management. When productive workers are denied their rightful rewards and unproductive workers are provided a free ride, the credibility of public programs is jeopardized, and public programs become vulnerable to criticisms and attacks from both inside and outside the organization.

The New York State Department of Civil Service developed a performance assessment process that assessed actual job performance. The assessment was used in conjunction with a second test component, usually a written test. In many instances, performance assessment scores were given a relative weight of two-thirds, and the traditional test scores a relative weight of one-third. A study of 42 examinations with a performance assessment component generated an average validity of .89 (Southworth 2006). The rankings on the eligible lists for these 42 examinations accounted for 79 percent of the variation in worker job performance, an increase of 67–75 percent over conventional examinations. These results dramatically improved the usefulness of the eligible lists, placing more high-performing candidates at the top of the eligible lists.

Evaluating worker performance is a critical part of managing all organizational performance. The best workers need to be properly rewarded, and problem employees need to be held accountable for their actions so the organization is able to demonstrate that high performance is important. The performance assessment process, presented in more detail later in the chapter, is a key tool to achieve this goal.

Assessments of Fairness

Fairness is the final work outcome presented in the WPF. Much of what is written in the U.S. Constitution addresses social justice, and social justice in many respects is synonymous with fairness. The structure of government was created to give the federal government certain duties and powers while preserving other rights and powers for the states. This structure was extended to the people by giving them broad freedoms to do what is not expressly limited or controlled by the federal and state governments.

Rasinski (1987) compares people's values about fairness with their underlying views of social justice. He refers to Deutsch's (1975) formulation that social goals of productivity, social harmony, and humanitarianism are addressed according to the principles of equity, equality, and need. Rasinski matches the concept of *proportionality* with equity, wherein distributive fairness means a person is rewarded according to her work contribution. He also aligns economic individualism with equity, so that the individual is responsible for her own economic well-being. He links the concept of *egalitarianism* with equality, wherein distributive fairness means benefits are distributed to people equally, and procedural fairness means that people have equal access to the decision process of distribution.

The WPF presents four components of fairness: (1) equity, (2) equality, (3) due process and the right to dissent, and (4) the social contract. Equity requires that individuals receive certain rewards and punishments based on their individual performance. Equality means that all people are entitled to certain benefits irrespective of their individual accomplishments. Due process and the right to dissent entitle a person, individually or through representation, to present objections about the distribution of benefits, punishments, and treatment based on claims of inequity or inequality. The social contract imposes the responsibility for being a good citizen on all people in return for the first three rights.

This concept of fairness addresses productivity and social harmony by assigning both equity and equality a rightful place in social systems. The relative importance of one over the other can vary according to the wishes of the citizens as determined through the election of their representatives.

Sometimes an extreme point is reached, where either equity or equality dominates, and our attention to the other is overlooked or undervalued. At that point, society reacts, and the pendulum swings the other way.

So, for example, when President Reagan confronted the air traffic controllers for attempting to shut down all the airways of the United States, the pendulum was perceived to have swung too far toward the worker. Today the pendulum has perhaps swung too far the other way, and the voices of dissent in favor of the worker—about the unfairness of globalization, for example, or the loss of job security—are being heard. This change in perceived fairness very likely affected the results of recent elections. Due process and the right to dissent are not limited to the courts or the press; they extend to the ballot box, as well, when we cast our votes for government leaders.

The principle of economic individualism, in which a person is responsible for her own economic condition, is valued by many people, while the principle of the social contract is not a prevalent theme in the American society. In Europe the social contract is very strong, but here we seem to prize individual freedom above the social contract. The WPF presents the social contract as the fourth component of fairness and social justice; it is a glaring omission of contemporary discussions in the United States and warrants greater research and exploration.

As laudable as the WPF's system of fairness is, it does not address the concepts of humanitarianism and need. People might be incapable of performing at a level that the marketplace demands, or they sometimes make disastrous mistakes, such as breaking laws or plunging into debt, and have difficulty making amends for their deeds. Consequently, there are two additional concepts that a fair society must understand and embrace—generosity and mercy. Generosity gives a gift to someone not for meritorious service but because she is in need, while mercy involves redemption or the forgiveness of improper activities or behaviors, and allows a person a second chance to do better.

All of these concepts of fairness are readily adapted to the organizational setting. In the private sector we can see a definite emphasis on equity and rewarding the worker for her individual performance. However, with the flattening of the organization and the promotion of the team environment, respect for one another and fair treatment have also gained prominent roles in the culture of organizations.

In the public sector, certain concerns for equality are especially important, such as treating constituents fairly, providing fair access to jobs, and providing workers with stability and good benefits. While concerns for equity that relate to finding the best workers and paying them well are becoming more important, the public sector will likely never match the level of interest of the private sector, which is driven by market forces. Since humanitarianism is fundamental to so many public-sector jobs and programs, the values that people have about equity and equality will likely influence their decisions about which sector to enter.

The Civil Rights Act of 1964 was perhaps the most important document to advance the cause of equal employment opportunity for all.* While some cases of overt discrimination in employment still exist, there have been enormous gains over the last 40 years. The underlying theme of the Act was equal treatment, i.e., disadvantaged minority populations cannot be discriminated against and must be given the same rights as the majority (generally represented as white males). Once laws that granted these rights were passed, people had access to due process procedures to correct injustices and receive payments for damages.

---

*A lengthy explanation of the history of The Civil Rights Act of 1964 can be found at the home page of the Equal Employment Opportunity Commission at www.eeoc.gov/abouteeoc/35th/thelaw/index.html (accessed September 27, 2008).

Another line of argument for equal treatment is that while disadvantaged minorities may have equal access to employment through civil service examinations, they have not received the same proportion of appointments and suffer an adverse impact from these examinations from low representation. Advocates for a diversified workforce and equal representation argue that when minorities are not equally represented as agents of the government, their groups are more likely to receive unequal services and benefits. Moreover, government as a whole gains a broader perspective about how best to serve all its citizens when there is a fully diverse government workforce.

Fairness is a complex topic, and standards of fairness change and evolve over time. Slanderous words toward minority populations, which were socially acceptable just a few decades ago, now seem unacceptably harsh and offensive. Due process and the right to dissent continue to expand as issues such as discrimination in employment are clarified and methods of communication change, such as Internet blogging and e-mails. The social contract will likely take on greater importance in the United States, particularly as our interests become more global. Nonetheless, the continuum between equity and equality is subject to change and reversal. While we do see gains in social benefits for all, we also see increased opportunities for people to differentiate themselves through specialization.

Outcomes should not be measured simply in program benefits or even in terms of risks and benefits; rather, they include the worker outcomes of rewards and punishments, and the accompanying new obligations and adversities. Furthermore, these outcomes must be based on credible performance measures and concerns for fairness in order to gain broad acceptance in the workplace.

HUMAN RERSOURCE PROGRAMS TO ADDRESS OUTCOMES

The WFP presents HR programs that address outcomes from three perspectives:

1. Employee and Program Performance

    - Personnel assessment

    - Organizational development and improvement

2. Rewards and Punishments

    - Payroll services

    - Employee benefits

    - Workers compensation

    - Employee recognition

    - Labor relations

3. Legal Requirements and Fairness

    - Personnel transactions

    - Affirmative action

Employee and Program Performance

Program and employee performance measurements are needed to evaluate the benefits and unintended consequences of a service, who contributed to program successes and failures, and who should be rewarded (or punished). Program and employee performance measures are not merely good ideas in theory; they are critical to the credibility of public programs and the public service as a whole. This chapter later presents key effectiveness measures for evaluating HR program performance and performance measures for evaluating worker performance, with an in-depth look at a performance assessment process used at the New York State Department of Civil Service.

Organizational development and improvement involves developing work processes that go beyond today's level of work production and performance standards to meet tomorrow's needs and standards. HR managers play an important role because they must understand the work processes involved with work improvements, help the organization evaluate worker performance, and help the organization obtain and develop staff with the knowledge, skills, and abilities (KSAs) to meet present work demands and build the foundation for tomorrow's workforce.

Rewards and Punishments

Several HR programs are directly involved with worker rewards and punishments. These include payroll services, employee benefits, workers' compensation, employee recognition, and labor relations.

HR payroll services determine salaries and withholdings used for issuing paychecks. Employee benefits activities include aiding and advising employees on health insurance, life insurance, workers' compensation claims, retirement accounts, and benefit options. Employee benefits can add as much as 50 percent of the employee's salary to her employment cost. Employee recognition activities include annual awards events, birthday parties, and celebrations for completing a work project or large assignment to demonstrate to the employee that she is respected and valued by the organization. Employee recognition is an important tool for building a strong work community.

Labor relations activities include negotiating labor contracts, developing policies and procedures based on contract agreements and legal requirements, overseeing disciplinary procedures, addressing grievances, and providing guidance and training to supervisors and managers on discipline, time and attendance issues, and grievances.

Legal Requirements and Fairness

Personnel transactions are the link between employee work and payment for services. In New York State government, the Department of Civil Service certifies that payrolls are in compliance with the Civil Service Law. When an employee is appointed, a personnel transaction that must be approved by the Civil Service Department is completed. Once the transaction is approved, no further approval is needed until a change in employment is made, such as a transfer to another position, a promotion, or a termination. For municipalities the responsibility for certifying payrolls falls upon the local civil service commission or personnel officer. While this process might appear to be "red tape," it affirms the legality of every employee's salary (generally prior to payment), avoiding fraud, abuse, and the need to reclaim unauthorized payments after the fact.

Affirmative action activities include efforts to recruit and hire members of minority groups that are underrepresented. When minorities are not proportionately represented as agents of the government, their groups are vulnerable to receiving fewer services and benefits than those fully represented. Through diversity, government gains a broader perspective about how best to serve all its citizens.

KEY PERFORMANCE MEASURES

The key performance measures addressed in this chapter are evaluating worker performance and assessing HR program effectiveness.

Evaluating Worker Performance

As the WPF evolved, it became apparent that assessing worker performance might be the most important activity in HR management. Rather than viewing HR managers as partners in building an effective organization, program managers often look at the civil service system as an impediment. This distrust can be directly attributed to the tenure protections granted to public employees at the end of the probationary term and to the low validity of civil service examinations. When productive workers are denied their rightful rewards and unproductive workers are provided a free ride, the credibility of public programs is jeopardized. Therefore, evaluating worker performance is critical to managing worker performance, and performance assessment as a component of civil service examinations is a key outcome measurement for determining promotions.

The performance assessment process described here was used for more than 40 New York State civil service examinations. It begins with candidates submitting a paper that explains their accomplishments over the preceding several years. Figure 7-2 presents four performance dimensions and sixteen subcategories that were used in the performance assessment process. They are deeply embedded in the WPF.

FIGURE 7-2 Performance Assessment Dimensions and Subcategories

Dimension 1 – Program and Special Project Management/Involvement
a) Candidate's role in the activity
b) Quality of work completed by candidate and staff
c) Quantity of work completed by candidate and staff
d) Difficulty/complexity of the work
e) Important achievements, impacts, or outcomes of the activity
Dimension 2 – Program and Product Improvements and Innovations
a) Improvements
b) Innovations
c) Effects of these changes

Dimension 3 – Customer Service and Relations
    a) Written/oral communication with customers and special communication
       challenges
    b) Client outreach and training activities
    c) Speeches and articles

Dimension 4 – Staff and Self Development
    a) Staff mentoring, OJT, formal training, and recruitment activities
    b) Building interpersonal relationships and a team environment among staff
    c) Self-development involving formal coursework or training programs,
       seminars, networking, and active involvement in professional organizations
    d) In-house training, including special assignments and work teams as self-
       development
    e) Relevant credentials such as degrees, licenses, and certificates

---

Dimension 1, "Program and Special Project Management/Involvement," addresses work-production activities by instructing the candidate to explain the quality and quantity of the work she produced, as well as the outcomes of the work. The dimension goes beyond general program activities to include special project activities. Dimension 2, which addresses program improvements and innovations, and Dimension 3, which addresses work behaviors and communication, assess the other work processes and outputs discussed in Chapters 5 and 6. Dimension 4, which relates to staff and self-development activities, aligns with the enabling activities in the WPF presented in Chapter 3.

Candidates are instructed to present their accomplishments in descending order of importance and to give the time period for each activity, the full-time equivalency they worked on each assignment, and the name of the person who can best verify their work. Most often, the verifier is the direct supervisor or the project manager of a special project.

Raters, who are usually a candidate's supervisors, are briefed on the assessment process and given a package containing the candidate's performance-assessment paper, a set of instructions, and rating sheets. Raters must verify the candidate's information through direct knowledge or by contacting past supervisors, project managers, or other people identified by the candidate who can verify the work. The raters evaluate each dimension and subcategory, and provide justification for their ratings. Review teams are then set up to review the raters' evaluations from a more global perspective to look for errors and decide whether a rater is being too hard or too lenient. After the eligibility list has been established, candidates may appeal their ratings to the State Civil Service Commission under an administrative appeal process.

A general industry guideline for interpreting the internal reliability of rater assessments is .90 and above (excellent), .80–.89 (good), .70–.79 (adequate) and below .70 (may have limited applicability) (HR-Guide. com 2008). The average internal reliability of the performance assessment rating sheets was .83. This figure is very high in light of the fact that the number of rating dimensions ranged from just 3 to 6, and on average there were just 26 candidates per examination.

A greater reliability concern is inter-rater reliability. Will two different raters award the same ratings? Particular concerns include inter-rater variation in rater severity and within-rater variation of rater severity (Wilson and Wang 1995), and halo errors (Fisicaro and Lance 1990), which were discussed in Chapter 2. Because of these concerns, improvements were frequently made to address rater reliability.

Perhaps the most important improvement to the performance assessment process was to require the candidates, instead of their raters, to explain and be fully responsible for documenting their work performance. When the raters are evaluating the candidate's papers, they may not provide additional information that could be used to raise the score above what the candidate's paper warrants. The second important improvement was the development of the four performance dimensions just discussed. Other changes to increase the reliability of the process follow:

- Require candidates to list their activities in descending order of importance, so the rater, the review panel, and the State Civil Service Commission agree on the candidate's most important work.

- Require candidates to provide specific information on the 16 sub-categories within the four performance dimensions. These sub-categories evolved over time. For example, difficulty/complexity of work was added as a subcategory for Dimension 1 to address cases of unfair scores for candidates who claimed to be high producers but were given easy assignments and limited responsibility.

- Allow the review panel to challenge the ratings, require the rater to provide more information, and even overrule the rater when appropriate.

- Use a single review panel to evaluate all candidates on one or more of the dimensions whenever possible, in order to address concerns about inter-review panel reliability. When this requirement is too burdensome, review panels are instructed to perform an analysis of the number of changes each panel has made to determine whether adjustments are needed.

The greatest problem associated with performance assessments is cost. The raters and review panels, who are generally the supervisors and managers of the candidates, spend a great deal of time on the process. Their time must be viewed as an expense. Also, there were many appeals that ultimately went to the State Civil Service Commission for adjudication. The preparation of the appeal packages and the work spent by the commission to review the appeals were burdensome, time-consuming, and costly.

Despite the marked increase in test validity and variance, it remains unclear whether performance assessment as a component of civil service examinations will gain greater acceptance. Low-performing workers are often contentious; they sometimes abuse the appeal process, which adds significantly to the administrative costs and makes the process more cumbersome than it needs to be. Nonetheless, accurately assessing worker performance is key to an effective HR program.

Assessing Human Resource Program Effectiveness

Figure 7-3 aligns the HR strategic objectives of building capacity, building performance, and building community with the service objectives of meeting the various needs of the organization. The figure also presents 21 performance measures for HR program effectiveness and the desired direction of each measure.

FIGURE 7-3 Effectiveness Measures for Human Resource Programs

Strategic Objectives	Service Objectives	Effectiveness Measures	Desired Direction
Building Capacity	Meeting the Staffing Needs	Change in # of right positions	Increase
		Change in # of wrong positions	Decrease
		Change in # of right staff	Increase
		Change in # of wrong staff	Decrease
	Meeting the Employee Development Needs	Change in KSAs	Increase
		Change in employee growth and development	Increase
Building Performance	Meeting the Performance Management Needs	Change in effort	Increase
		Change in power	Increase
		Change in processes and systems	Better
		Change in outputs	Better
		Change in HR program benefits	Better
		Change in risks and unintended consequences	Decrease
	Meet the Diversity, Compliance and Fairness Needs	Change in assessment of performance	Better
		Change in diversity	Increase
		Change in fairness	Increase
Building Community	Meeting the Employee Rewards and Benefits Needs	Change in rewards	Increase
		Change in punishments	Decrease
		Change in adversities and obligations	Decrease
		Change in employee-job fit	Increase
	Meeting the Work Environment Needs	Change in employee satisfaction	Increase
		Change in employee vitality and well-being	Increase
		Change in stakeholder satisfaction	Increase

Performance measures for building HR capacity focus on (1) meeting the organization's staffing needs by increasing the number of positions needed for the new work environment and the number of staff to fill these positions and by decreasing the number of obsolete positions and staff whose KSAs are no longer needed and who cannot be trained; and (2) meeting staff training and development needs by increasing the KSAs of those who can be trained.

To develop a useful survey, program managers must know what people and positions they now have, which ones they need, and which ones they could do without. They must also know which KSAs are needed to complete the work, and the competence of their staff. The HR manager plays a key role in working with the program managers to develop and address this workforce planning information.

Performance measures for building HR performance focus on meeting the organizational performance needs of increasing or improving inputs, processes, outputs, and positive outcomes, as well as decreasing negative outcomes such as risks, unintended consequences, adversities, and punishments. Performance measures for building HR performance must also address other outcomes related to employee benefits, diversity, fairness, and legal compliance.

Performance measures for building community indicate the effectiveness of the work environment in establishing trust, affiliation, and a sense of a greater good within the organization. Measures of effectiveness include increases in employee satisfaction and well-being, and the satisfaction of other stakeholders.

As discussed in Chapter 2, measuring HR capacity, performance, and community can be achieved by:

- Measuring the efficiency of HR programs

- Monitoring organizational effectiveness from reports by the operating divisions on program performance
- Asking the operating divisions directly or with a survey
- Asking the employees directly or with a survey
- Asking your HR staff directly or with a survey.

Surveys of program managers, employees, stakeholders, and HR staff serve as a feedback loop for vital information on the effectiveness of program services, while production reports can be used to measure outputs and confirm the claims of effectiveness or ineffectiveness.

THE FUTURE STATE OF HUMAN RESOURCE MANAGEMENT AND RESEARCH OPPORTUNITIES

Researchers and public administrators have given a great deal of attention to outcomes, but their focus has largely been on benefits, with less attention to risks. The WPF presents rewards, punishments, obligations, and adversities as outcomes for the worker, and including these concepts as outcomes provides great opportunities for researchers to test and develop hypotheses. The WPF also presents performance measures and fairness as outcomes, revealing the huge gap in HR literature and research when practitioners try to find baseline measures and benchmarks and discover they are not readily available. This omission is particularly dramatic when compared to private industry's detailed measures of products, production activities, and customer interests.

Globally, the WPF's proposal that building capacity, performance, and community is the fundamental purpose of HR programs will serve as focal points for researchers and HR managers as they seek to refine HR service measures and guide improvements. HR managers in the public sector have long understood the value of building community, but they have been less attuned to building capacity and performance. Civil service examinations have been the necessary evil for staffing public programs because most people believe that without them political leaders would return to some form of a spoils system. But the problems with civil service examinations are well understood, and some jurisdictions have reduced civil service requirements or eliminated them entirely. Undoubtedly, some form of worker performance assessment, which is tied to organizational performance, is needed in the public sector to raise its credibility.

There are a number of opportunities for future research, and they will likely form around building capacity, performance, and community. First, the distinction between effort and motivation will clarify how people act as HR inputs. Perseverance and handling adversities are areas that are ripe for research coverage. This research should provide ways for organizations to prepare their future leaders for the demands of working in high-level positions. It should also bring light to how organizations can reduce adversities that are preventable, particularly personality conflicts that infect worker enthusiasm and job satisfaction.

Finally, there needs to be greater attention to the concept of fairness as a balance between rewarding the individual for her individual performance and building a community where everyone benefits. This is especially relevant to diversity and group representation. Moreover, the concepts of generosity and mercy need to be better understood in terms of what they mean, how they are carried out, and what effects they have on the recipients and the benefactors.

The effectiveness measures presented in this chapter will lead to a greater understanding of what must be done to build effective HR programs. By closely evaluating and acting on these measures, researchers and HR managers will be able to provide the greatly needed data and performance benchmarks.

If there is one point to be emphasized in this chapter, it is that outcomes involve much more than program benefits. Outcomes also include failures and missed opportunities; the rewards and punishments workers receive from their work contributions; the obligations and adversities that come with accepting an appointment or promotion; the measurement and evaluation of people and programs that determine who is rewarded and what changes must be made; and the fairness of public programs in addressing the various needs and interests of the program recipients, employees, and other stakeholders.

In addition to increasing organizational performance, program managers must increase organizational capacity, especially technology capacity and HR capacity, to meet future challenges and embrace future opportunities. Linking greater HR capacity to greater organizational capacity makes the HR manager a vital strategic partner within the organization. The WPF is a tool for the HR manager to assess present HR performance and develop a strategic plan for workforce improvement through improved staffing programs, improved employee-development programs, improved performance-management programs, improved rewards and benefits, a better work environment, and improved legal and procedural requirements based on fairness considerations.

Impacts

I mpacts are the reactions by people—customers, employees, and other stakeholders—to work systems, outputs, and outcomes. They are the domain of the industrial psychologists, satisfaction surveys, polls, and choices. What do I feel? What are my judgments? What are my beliefs? What am I going to do? How am I going to vote? This chapter merges the selected literature review with the background information on impacts in the Work Performance Framework (WPF) because they are so closely intertwined. It then looks at the related HR programs and key measures, followed by a discussion of future issues in HR management and research opportunities. The chapter concludes by revisiting the question, What makes a good worker?

IMPACTS IN THE WORK PERFORMANCE FRAMEWORK

The WPF presents four categories of impacts: emotional, psychological, spiritual, and intellectual. (See Figure 8-1, "Work Performance Framework—Impacts.") Emotional impacts are the emotions and feelings we experience in reaction to system variables; psychological impacts are our attitudinal reactions; spiritual impacts are the reactions to our state of well-being derived from these experiences; and intellectual impacts are the changes in our beliefs, developed from our experiences within the entire work performance system from beginning to end.

FIGURE 8-1 Work Performance Framework—Impacts

IMPACTS	DETAILS
<u>Emotional</u> Feelings	*Affiliation* Security Pleasure Empathy Achievement
<u>Psychological</u> Attitudes Judgments	*Trust* *Esteem* <u>Ethics</u> Self-interest Benevolence Principles <u>Fairness</u> Equity Equality Due Process, Right to Dissent Social Contract
<u>Intellectual</u> Reasoning Beliefs	*Meaning* Effectiveness Efficiency Reliability
<u>Spiritual</u> Well-being	*Happiness* *Comfort* *Involvement*

The WPF posits that intelligence is different from our general mental ability and personality. Intelligence is not a human resource, but rather a compilation of beliefs about all we are, all we do, and all we experience. With these beliefs, we make myriad decisions as we live our lives. Just as we learn about other people from the decisions they make, they learn who we are from our decisions; they develop their own beliefs about us; and they decide how they will interact with us.

The emotional, intellectual, and psychological impacts roughly parallel Freud's mental structure of the id, the ego, and the superego, while the spiritual impact addresses our state of well-being. While Freud put great stock in the superego, or our self-judgments, the dominant impact in the WPF is intellectual, because the intellect takes into consideration our feelings, attitudes, and sense of well-being as we develop beliefs for making decisions.

As discussed in Chapter 6, the output of work behaviors is interpersonal communication, which is used to build trust and affiliation. Affiliation is achieved by positively connecting with another person's emotions, whereas trust is achieved by positively connecting with another person's psychological judgments or attitudes. To understand effective interpersonal communication, it is important to understand emotional and psychological impacts because these are our personal reactions to interpersonal communication.

EMOTIONAL IMPACTS

Emotional impacts are reactions related to our terminal values that affect our feelings and address our wants and needs. Emotional impacts address the question, What is it we are looking for in life?

Selected Literature Review

Rokeach and Ball-Rokeach (1989) discuss stability and change in American values during the period from 1968 to 1981 based on the Rokeach Value Survey (Rokeach 1967), or RVS. The RVS contains two sets of values: 18 *instrumental* values and 18 *terminal* values. Instrumental values are standards that apply to how we achieve desired outcomes, while terminal values assess the outcomes.

Rokeach and Ball-Rokeach report results of surveys on terminal values in 1968, 1971, 1974, and 1981, and the results of 1968 and 1971 surveys on instrumental values. Of the 18 terminal values, "a world at peace" and "family security" ranked either first or second in all four surveys, while "freedom" ranked third in all four surveys.

Using regression analysis of terminal values in the RVS and other surveys, including the list of values presented by Kahle (1983), Kamakura and Novak (1992) identified four value domains common to terminal values: hedonism (pleasure), empathy (human relations), achievement, and security. They reported that hedonism, empathy, and achievement represented distinct motivational forces, whereas security tended to negate these forces.

When they applied their findings to more than 80 consumer activities, security interests tended to generate few significant correlations with these activities, and those that did yield significant correlations with security were negative, signifying avoidance. Just two activities that generated positive correlations with security: (1) eating white bread and (2) watching quiz and audience shows on television. This suggests that security is not so much a motivating force as a demotivating force.

This literature is significant in explaining why individuals react differently to different organizations and to other people, why they have different interests, and why they seek different life goals. It also suggests a negative side of security as a goal, that of goal inhibitor.

Emotional Impacts in the Work Performance Framework

Figure 8-1 includes Kamakura and Novak's value domains of security, pleasure, empathy, and achievement as the underlying domains of terminal values associated with emotions in the WPF. It is easy to see the strong emotional connections we make with these terms by looking at their antonyms: pain (the opposite of pleasure), loneliness (empathy or human relations), failure (achievement), and fear/anger (security). It is relevant to note that failure as a motivator likely plays a central role in work performance, in the work environment, and in the WPF.

Maslow describes a hierarchy of needs beginning with physiological needs and advancing to needs of safety, love and belonging, esteem, and self-actualization. The WPF does not view the four value domains as hierarchical, although similarities to Maslow's needs are evident, with security interests representing safety, empathy representing love and belonging, and pleasure and achievement representing esteem and self-actualization.

Cacioppo and Gardner (1999) note that in the past emotions were deemed a disruptive force in rational thought, but contemporary discussions of "emotional intelligence" make the case that emotions are a valuable force, contributing to a greater fullness of life. These discourses on emotions, however, appear to concentrate on empathy and establishing interpersonal relationships. While empathy is represented by work behaviors (processes), interpersonal communication (outputs), and the intrinsic benefits of the work environment (outcomes) in the WPF, it accounts for just one of the four emotional impacts. This suggests that there are significant opportunities to pursue other lines of inquiry related to emotional impacts, particularly those related to achievement and failure.

The findings of Cacioppo and Gardner suggest that feelings or emotional impacts play an integral role in intelligence and intelligent decision-making (intellectual impacts in the WPF). However, people vary dramatically in their terminal values and the level of importance they give to their emotions and feelings when making decisions.

When people lose control of their decision-making abilities because of uncontrollable emotional reactions, they are said to be making "rash" decisions. Of course, we are all overcome with rage, grief, and remorse at some time or another, but when everyday events arouse strong emotional reactions, a person may have trouble making even routine decisions. Over time, intense feelings usually subside.

Often, overriding emotional reactions are the result of chemical reactions within the body, prompting the growing use of medications to treat these emotional problems, sometimes effectively, and unfortunately, sometimes unnecessarily. Despite the problems we might experience from our emotions, they also provide our greatest rewards in life, and our terminal values direct us toward our life goals.

Work Culture

Within the organization, terminal values are seen in the work culture of the people in the organization. For example, do they display empathy? Is the culture of the organization dominated by a drive to achieve excellence in the quality of its products and services? Is the organization highly protective of its existence and its present state? While organizations may focus on just one or two terminal values when describing or constructing their work culture, these four value domains are universal, so they all need to be represented in the work culture to some degree.

PSYCHOLOGICAL IMPACTS

Psychological impacts address three key areas of uncertainty: motivations, processes, and distributions. Motivational uncertainties are evaluated according to the ethical criteria of self-interest, benevolence, and principles, while procedural and distributive uncertainties are evaluated according to the fairness criteria discussed in Chapter 7.

While emotions and feelings are tied to affiliation within the WPF and based on terminal values, psychological impacts are judgments and attitudes of trust and esteem based on instrumental values. Instrumental values answer the question "How?" How will I achieve the goals that will satisfy my terminal values? Of Rokeach's 18 instrumental values, the top three values for both the 1968 and 1971 surveys were honesty, ambition, and responsibility.

Figure 8-2 presents ten essential virtues listed on the website of the Maxwell School at Syracuse University (Lickona 2004).

FIGURE 8-2 Virtues

| Wisdom |
| Justice |
| Fortitude |
| Self-mastery |
| Love |
| Positive Attitude |
| Hard Work |
| Integrity |
| Gratitude |
| Humility |

Lickona expands on the meaning of these virtues. For example, wisdom involves "Moral and intellectual discernment: Telling right from wrong, truth from falsehood, fact from opinion, the eternal from the transitory" and "Understanding human nature (e.g., the need to feel valued and significant)." Virtues can be looked at as instrumental values because they answer the question about how to go about living one's life.

Rokeach's lists of values and Lickona's virtues are not consistent with the WPF. For example, Rokeach lists loving as an instrumental value and love as a terminal value. Lickona lists love as a virtue that includes empathy, compassion, kindness, selfless generosity, service, loyalty, patriotism, and forgiveness. The WPF views love as a terminal value under the value domain of empathy or human relations because love is an end unto itself. However, we present the ethical criterion of benevolence as instrumental because it addresses how to act in order to build a trusting relationship.

Attitudes

The WPF presents an attitude as a heuristic, psychological device to provide and communicate swift judgments on expectations about uncertain outcomes based on levels of trust and esteem. While feelings are reactions to the benefits of outputs, attitudes are reactions to their uncertainty. Since attitudes are public behaviors, they can evoke strong reactions from other people, even when they are unintentional.

When a person remarks, "I don't like your attitude toward me," she means, "I don't like your judging me as untrustworthy or holding me in low esteem." When we think that a person's attitude toward work is not good, the conclusion should be based on the person's work conduct and compliance with work standards, not her life aspirations.

Attitudes can be well-founded or instinctive. While an attitude can be viewed as a biased evaluation or predisposition, it is particularly useful in situations where quick decisions are needed. Attitudes are not meant to replace rational judgments and decision-making when greater time and resources are available. Unfortunately, because they are so accessible, attitudes are often wrongly used in place of wiser judgments derived from more extensive investigation. Still, attitudes that were formed over many years can be highly reliable and useful.

Attitudes can be positive or negative and persist for long times depending on their usefulness in past situations. Attitude change has been a popular topic for researchers. Petty et al. (1997) discuss a number of issues associated with attitude change. One of these is "mere exposure," which explains that the more a person is exposed to something or someone, the more familiar and trusting he becomes. This theory is relevant for advertising—the more a person sees a product, the more likely he is to trust it and want to purchase it.

Within the workplace, exposure can be very helpful in developing interpersonal relations and gaining trust, so people assigned to field positions or "backroom" jobs might find their work underappreciated and undervalued due to the lack of exposure. While many workers might prefer working by themselves, they might be passed over for promotions for failing to pursue opportunities to build trusting relationships with the people making the promotion decisions.

Another popular strategy to build positive attitudes is conditioning, where positive experiences are used in association with a product or during a group work assignment to create a positive conditioned response. Simple rewards such as a compliment on a recent job assignment can be very helpful to a supervisor or manager in building a relationship with his staff. Conversely, when workers make unfavorable impressions during group assignments, they may be creating negative conditioned responses without knowing it, leading to unfavorable attitudes that undermine trust and their hopes for that next promotion.

Ethical Criteria and Judgments

Ethical evaluation is an important aspect of psychological judgments and attitudes. Victor and Cullen (1988) present a matrix of nine possible climate types based on three ethical criteria (egoism [self-interest], benevolence, and principles) matched against three loci of analysis (individual, local [organization], and cosmopolitan [society]). By performing a rotated factor analysis, they identified five ethical work climates within the organizations they studied: (1) caring, (2) law and code, (3) rules, (4) instrumental, and (5) independence.

The work climate of a Type 1 organization is dominated by the ethical criterion of benevolence or concern for others. The work climates of Type 2 and Type 3 organizations are dominated by concerns for principles. The work climate of a Type 4 organization is dominated by concerns for egoism or self-interest, and the work climate of a Type 5 organization is dominated by workers acting responsibly according to whatever ethical criteria they deem best for the situation.

One can easily imagine how a person whose terminal values and emotions are strongly tied to empathy can develop an ethical preference to benevolence over principles or self-interest. Another person whose terminal values and emotions are most strongly based in achievement may prefer the ethical criterion of self-interest and, perhaps, principles to ensure a level playing field. Many sports are characterized by the terminal value of achievement and the instrumental values of self-interest (winning), along with principles (playing by the rules of the game). Thus ethical criteria are critical for how we judge people and events; they directly affect our attitudes and are closely associated with our instrumental and terminal values.

Fairness and Social Justice

As previously discussed, the WPF proposes that there are four essential components of fairness and social justice: equity, equality, due process and the right to dissent, and the social contract. Two primary areas of concern pertaining to fairness and justice affect our psychological judgments: *distributive* justice and *procedural* justice.

Distributive justice addresses results or outcomes. Were the results fair? Distributive justice addresses both equity (better results or rewards based on better inputs or performance) and equality (substantial common benefits for all). Because equity and equality are placed on opposite ends of a continuum, the challenge for accomplishing a fair and just outcome is balancing concerns for equity against concerns for equality. Moreover, because economic conditions and political viewpoints change, there are regular shifts in popular support for how benefits should be distributed.

Message framing and interpretation are important aspects of distributive justice. Message framing refers to how the result or outcome is presented. A positive message would be framed as a benefit, such as living on a cleaner planet or saving money on the price of fuel, whereas a negative message would be framed as avoiding a global disaster from warming of the planet caused by burning fossil fuels.

Message interpretation refers to how people understand a message, and it can vary based on people's self-concept and expectations. As mentioned in Chapter 7, people tend to be risk-averse when the outcome is seen as a gain or benefit, but risk-prone when the outcome is seen as a loss. When a person expects a reward but does not get it, he might interpret the result as a loss, whereas when a person is not expecting a reward, he might look at any reward as a gain.

A classic challenge in HR management is selecting one person for promotion and explaining to another hard-working person why he was not promoted, so he does not misinterpret the event as a loss. Another challenge is to constructively criticize performance and have the worker accept constructive criticism well. When a person interprets criticism or being passed over for promotion as punishment or a loss, he is more likely to become upset and react poorly. Negative reactions can affect a worker's willingness to abide by the social contract of being a good worker, so it is very important to understand how people might react to events and take steps to ameliorate the situation.

Procedural justice addresses due process and the right to dissent. Negative reactions based on procedural injustice can also affect a worker's willingness to abide by the social contract of being a good worker. Miller (2001) reports that procedural justice is the most popular topic in justice research over the last two decades. Two aspects of procedural justice have emerged as important and are now regarded as entitlements: (1) showing respect and (2) providing a voice, or the opportunity to speak on one's own behalf. The right to respectful treatment during fairness and justice procedures parallels the right to positive work behaviors in the work environment. "Voice" is fundamental to the concepts of due process and the right to dissent.

Miller notes that accountability is also fundamental to procedural justice and "people think they are entitled to explanations and accounts for any actions that have personal consequences for them (Bies and Shapiro 1987; Bobocel et al. 1998; Shapiro et al. 1994)" (531). Still, full transparency is difficult to accomplish in an organizational setting, and people who are given the right to make their case or dissent often abuse these rights by pursuing their own interests long after an issue has been adjudicated.

Work Climate

Victor and Cullen evaluated the organizational work climate based on ethical criteria. Attitudes about one's organization and organizational work climate are based on instrumental values as opposed to terminal values. Fairness and social justice considerations play important roles in affecting our psychological judgments of how, and how well, an organization operates. Making the distinction between work climate and work culture might seem like hair-splitting, but it is helpful to show that the way people behave in an organization based on their instrumental values is as important as, but different from, what they seek to pursue based on their terminal values.

SPIRITUAL IMPACTS

The WPF presents well-being as a spiritual impact, as distinguished from emotional, attitudinal, and intellectual impacts. Well-being is the measurement of mental and physical health of the individual that addresses the question "How much?" How much am I benefiting from my emotions and attitudes? Although the physical health of the body and mind is relevant to well-being, it is not the focus of this section, since physical ailments are treated by medical professionals. Spiritual impact is also not addressed here from a theological perspective, although it is discussed to some extent in the professional literature.

Selected Literature Review

Ryan and Deci (2001) and Diener et al. (2003) reviewed the existing literature on well-being. Ryan and Deci explored the distinction between hedonic and eudaimonic aspects of well-being, while Diener et al. discussed personality and cultural influences on subjective well-being. The following review provides insights into well-being and exposes some unresolved concerns.

Ryan and Deci note that well-being is an important topic because it addresses the issues of what constitutes "the good life" and how to optimize this experience within the various societal institutions, including government, therapy, and education. In the 1960s the focus of well-being shifted from preventing problems to promoting and maximizing well-being in society. In this context, well-being includes growth, well-being, and wellness.

Two areas of interest to well-being were forged: hedonism, which holds that well-being consists of happiness and pleasure, and eudaimonism, which is the actualization of human potential. Discussions of hedonistic well-being evolved into subjective well-being (Diener and Lucas 1999), consisting of three components: life satisfaction, presence of positive mood, and absence of negative mood.

Ryan and Deci note that eudaimonism is derived from the concept that people must live according to their *daimon,* or true self (Waterman 1993). Thus well-being involves more than happiness and includes the pursuit of values beyond pleasure. In this regard, a measure of well-being is vitality or the thirst for living rather than just happiness and pleasure. Autonomy was identified as a strong contributor to vitality.

Diener et al. (2003) discuss the relationship of personality and culture to subjective well-being (SWB). Their description of SWB involves "how people evaluate their lives . . . their emotional reactions to events, their moods, and judgments they form about life satisfaction, fulfillment, and satisfaction with domains such as marriage and work" (404).

The emotional component of SWB measures feelings of joy and contentment, while the cognitive component measures general life satisfactions and specific satisfaction with domains such as marriage, work, and leisure.

Diener et al. note that studies have linked elements of the "big five" personality traits to SWB—extraversion, emotional stability, conscientiousness, agreeableness, and openness to experience. Extraversion formed a positive association with SWB, while neuroticism formed a negative association. To a lesser extent, agreeableness and conscientiousness correlated with SWB as well. They also note that richer countries generally experienced greater levels of SWB, but wealth is not as significant a factor in SWB in those nations. This suggests that lack of income is an obstacle to well-being, but wealth is perhaps only a moderate factor in contributing to well-being once a certain income level is attained.

Diener et al. also note that European Americans were significantly more satisfied with their lives than Asians and Asian Americans. They also note that European Americans were more likely than Asian Americans to switch to another task when they did not do well. European Americans were also less happy than were Asian Americans when engaging in activities related to future goals as opposed to what is important at the moment. This led Diener et al. to question "whether achieving these other goals ultimately leads to higher levels of life satisfaction even though positive moods might be sacrificed in the short run" (413).

Three important issues need to be reconciled to clarify the meaning of well-being within the context of the WPF: (1) distinctions between happiness and pleasure as components of hedonism; (2) distinctions between happiness and well-being; and (3) distinctions between well-being and subjective well-being.

Distinctions between Happiness and Pleasure

Happiness and *pleasure* are terms that appear to be almost synonymous in general parlance, and both terms are associated with the concept of hedonism. Kamakura and Novak (1992) labeled one of the value segmentations they identified through regression analysis as hedonism, but it is interpreted in the WPF as pleasure.

Kamakura and Novak associated the concepts of fun, excitement, and enjoyment with the value segmentation of hedonism and reported that people who associated with this value segmentation tended to be young. Activities that they identified as correlating with hedonism include "browse in a bookstore," "play tennis," "use a sauna/hot tub," and "watch the television program 'Cheers.'" The WPF associates these activities with leisure time, so it substitutes the term pleasure for hedonism.

Happiness, on the other hand, is clearly related to our state of well-being and encompasses more than just pursuing fun and excitement and other acts of pleasure. This raises the second distinction, the difference between happiness and well-being.

Distinctions between Happiness and Well-being

The WPF presents three aspects of well-being in Figure 8-1: happiness, comfort, and involvement. As with emotional impacts, the antonyms of these components reinforce their relevance to the topic of well-being—sadness (happiness); stress and disorientation (comfort); and boredom, fatigue, and disenfranchisement (involvement). Since higher levels of involvement can, at times, reduce levels of happiness and comfort, well-being is not limited to happiness alone. It is achieved by balancing the three factors.

Happiness is one part of well-being, but it may not be its most important aspect. For some people, the greatest sense of well-being comes from total commitment to their work or family. Therefore the best indicator of well-being is vitality, mentioned earlier, because this term accommodates happiness, comfort, and involvement. Autonomy, which was identified as a strong contributor to vitality, is significant because it enables the individual to seek his own levels of happiness, comfort, and involvement in pursuit of well-being.

Comfort might be considered a subcomponent of happiness, but the WPF makes a distinction because comfort relates to issues of stress or disorientation. Stress is a negative reaction to an adversity, and workplace adversities can come in the forms of dangers, time constraints, and conflicts.

Dissonance (sometimes called cognitive dissonance) is a particular form of stress involving a conflict between a person's instrumental values, terminal values, or both.

Emotional dissonance is created by a conflict between competing terminal values or underlying value domains such as empathy and achievement. A person might experience dissonance by having to choose between a large family with many children or a highly successful career.

Psychological dissonance occurs when there are conflicts between competing instrumental values associated with trust and esteem. For example, a person whose dominant ethical criterion is benevolence may feel stress when his work involves disapproving a customer's request for a loan because certain criteria were not met.

Dissonance can just as easily arise when a person whose dominant ethical criterion is adherence to principles, rules, and regulations works in a human services organization helping people who are in desperate need but keep violating rules and requirements for service coverage. Mixed dissonance involves conflicts with both terminal and instrumental values. Thus someone can care very much for his child but experience dissonance because of events that make him distrustful of the child.

Disorientation is a state of not properly perceiving events and situations. Disorientation can be a sign of fatigue or the result of a larger emotional, psychological, or medical problem.

Involvement, the third component of well-being, can lead to some unhappiness and discomfort when pursued to the extreme. Some people believe that if you're happy and comfortable, you are not working hard enough or challenging yourself to reach a higher plateau. Achieving success generally involves additional work and more challenging responsibilities, including dealing with greater adversities. While too much adversity can lead to fatigue, avoiding adversities can lead to less involvement in work activities, resulting in boredom and even disenfranchisement.

The answer to the question raised by Diener et al.—whether foregoing short-term comfort can lead to deeper long-term life satisfaction—might be yes or no. In the short run, a person might simply prefer high involvement over comfort. In the long run, however, a person might never achieve the kind of well-being that comes with comfort because he always seeks challenges, conflicts, and dangers to overcome. On the other hand, he might at some point later in life find a deeper level of satisfaction and fulfillment from having lived a vigorous life.

Adversities can come from outside the workplace as well as from within. When a person has a great deal of stress dealing with adversities in his personal life, he may not be able to handle additional adversities at work. For this reason, employee assistance programs have become popular to help people deal with problems outside the workplace, especially problems of alcoholism and drug addiction.

For the HR manager, there are two important ways to address adversities in the workplace. First, he can reduce adversities by, for example, having guidelines for work behaviors at meetings that instruct participants to be respectful of other people's views and suggestions in order to reduce personality conflicts. Second, he can provide training and strategies in such areas as conflict management and time management.

Moods, both positive and negative, are considered a temporary state that can fluctuate or dissipate, sometimes quickly. Negative moods can signal a state of discomfort due to adversities, remorse from the failure to achieve important goals, or grief from the illness or loss of a dear friend or family member. Sometimes, moods are the result of a physical ailment that requires a medical solution, even though the person might give the impression that he is upset with a life experience.

Generally, a healthy, positive person is able to overcome an adversity in a relatively short time and regain his positive outlook. Sometimes, however, devastating events happen, and a negative mood can last a long time or never completely dissipate. These moods are especially important because they can adversely affect a person's perceptions, judgments, and decisions and can infect an organization's work culture or work climate.

Distinctions between Well-being and Subjective Well-being

The WPF's third distinction is between well-being and subjective well-being. As mentioned, the measurement instrument for subjective well-being described by Diener et al. contains an emotional component for feelings of joy and contentment and a cognitive component for satisfaction with our lives. The WPF limits well-being to the emotional component.

The cognitive component of subjective well-being is an intellectual impact because a person contemplates his state or condition of well-being and develops beliefs that influence his decisions on future actions. This same intellectual process takes place in assessing one's psychological impacts or attitudes as well as one's emotional impacts or feelings. The intellect uses these assessments to develop beliefs and make future decisions. The intellect can help us adjust our emotional state by understanding ourselves, other people, and our environment.

INTELLECTUAL IMPACTS

Intellectual impact is the fourth impact. The intellectual impact addresses the question, Why? Why do we do what we do? What should we do differently in the future? In one important way, the intellectual impact is the most important impact of all. We use our powers of reason to understand and explain our feelings, attitudes, and state of well-being so that we can make the best use of these intuitive resources when needed. From this understanding we develop beliefs about ourselves, other people, our environment, and the situations we experience.

While the WPF relates terminal values to emotions, our emotions do not perceive terminal values; they experience feelings that display positive and negative levels of affiliation with people or situations. While the WPF relates instrumental values to our psychological judgments, our psychological judgments do not perceive instrumental values; rather, they experience attitudes that display positive or negative levels of trust with people or situations. It is our intellect that makes sense out of our feelings and attitudes, and develops beliefs and heuristic models based on terminal values and instrumental values.

In the same way, our spiritual self does not evaluate whether we are happy, comfortable, or involved; it experiences our mental and physical condition and displays well-being through moods, dispositions, and levels of vitality. Our intellect makes sense of our state of well-being by developing theories and beliefs about the various types of conditions associated with well-being, causes and treatments for ailments, and strategies to exploit opportunities to improve our well-being.

What is an intellectual impact? Simply stated, it is a reaction to people and events through reasoning in order to develop beliefs and complex judgments, and to make decisions. During this process, our intellectual self considers our beliefs, emotions, attitudes, and state of well-being as factors for making decisions.

While one might argue that very often our emotions or attitudes decide our actions, within the WPF it is the intellect that has the capacity to override our feelings and attitudes through reasoning to make the best decisions. If an emotion is allowed to override our beliefs and intellectual decisions, it is because our intellect has permitted the override. Occasionally, of course, an emotion is too overpowering, but controlling our emotions and our attitudes is a discipline we learn at an early age. This control includes not only restraint but also effective use of our emotions and attitudes in building affiliations and trust, and experiencing life satisfaction. When a chemical reaction or mental or physical disorder prevents an intellectual response, therapy or other medical solutions may be needed.

A great deal of the literature focuses on thinking, reasoning, and decision-making to help explain and understand intellectual impacts. Markman and Gentner (2001) view thinking as a broader term than reasoning for the purpose of arriving at new conclusions, and they survey trends that include categorization, mental models, cognitive development, and decision-making. They note that reasoning is generally approached from two perspectives. The first perspective is abstract logical reasoning, which is applicable without any knowledge of the contents of a given situation, and the second is domain-specific reasoning, where thought is applied according to the contents of the situation.

In addition to a logical mental model, people construct causal mental models involving causal systems. The center of the WPF is a causal system of inputs-processes-outputs, but this center is preceded by antecedents of human resources and enablers, and followed by action-reaction systems involving outcomes and impacts. The WPF represents what Markman and Gentner call scripts, which are general belief structures with "chiefly linear temporal order with inferential flexibility" (231).

Using reasoning, people form judgments and make decisions. Shafir and LeBoeuf (2002) discuss "probability judgments," in which people evaluate the likelihood of their judgment's being correct. When probabilities are not well calibrated, people are more likely to make poor decisions. Because judgments often rely on a number of different attributes, each probability judgment can reduce the probability of the final decision.

Shafir and LeBoeuf report that people have poor insights into how much to weigh each attribute. For example, in HR management, people must evaluate the attributes of a job applicant to predict whether he will be an effective worker. People also weigh the probability of their benefiting from a decision. As discussed in Chapter 7, expected utility theory deals with probabilities of benefits against the value of the benefit, while prospect theory deals with probability versus overall results.

In an economic model, people weigh financial benefits of an action against the likelihood of the action's succeeding. Herbert Simon, however, famously posited that due to time constraints and interest people act by "satisficing," or satisfying certain conditions rather than considering every possible financial alternative. While there might be a better deal out there, it may not be worth the additional investment of time and effort to make the best deal. Moreover, while wealth is a contributor to well-being, the importance of economic benefits, on average, diminishes once a person has attained a certain level of wealth and comfort. Thus the pure economic model is impractical, and economics as a sole criterion for decision-making is incomplete.

Mellers et al. (1998) describe several aspects of decision-making. They note that March (1994) divides decision-making into preference-based choices and rule following. Mellers et al. note that preference-based decision-making has been explored more fully based on beliefs and values, while "rule following involves the application of rules or principles to situations." For rule-based decisions, they cite Fiske (1992), who classifies social decisions under four categories of rules: communal sharing, authority ranking, equality matching, and market pricing. Mellers et al. note that reason-based choices may be made using lists of pros and cons, or take the form of stories.

Regarding preference-based choices, Mellers et al. expand perceptions of risk to include pre-decision affect (How do I feel at the time of the decision?) and post-decision affect (How will I feel after the decision?) as influences on decision-making. Emotional perceptions of risk are presented in terms of "dread, lack of familiarity, and lack of controllability" (Fischhoff et al. 1981). They also discuss various elements of preference-based choices, including beliefs and probabilistic judgments, and refer to Bayesian belief networks that "consist of nodes, representing probabilistic variables, and links, representing relations between nodes" that are used to map preferences.

Edwards and Fasolo (2001) delve further into the decision-making processes by raising three key questions: How do people go about making decisions? How should people go about making decisions? What is the best decision, and how can the decision maker find, recognize, and implement it? (Edwards and Fasolo, 582). Since there has been ample discussion of the first question, they concentrated on addressing the other two.

To begin, they outline three rules—multi-attribute utility (MAU) measurements, Bayes' theorem of probability theory, and maximization of subjectively expected utility (Max SEU). In this process, values and rewards of all types (multi-attributive utility) are converted to numerical values so probability and value of outcomes can be determined and combined to calculate the best decision. The Bayesian model, just discussed, is used to map out preferences. The third rule is stated as (Edwards and Fasolo, 585):

1. In the rare situation in which you have no uncertainty about outcomes of any available act, choose the act with the highest utility.

2. In decision under uncertainty, choose the act with the highest SEU.

From these three rules, Edwards and Fasolo constructed a decision-making process that includes 19 steps, which are presented in Figure 8-3.

FIGURE 8-3 Nineteen Steps to a Decision*

Steps	Tasks
1	Identify options
2	Identify possible outcomes of each option
3	Identify attributes with which to evaluate outcomes
4	Score each outcome on each attribute
5	Weight attributes
6	Aggregate scores and weights into utilities (MAU)
7	Identify events that determine which outcomes will follow choice of an option
8	For each event, specify a prior distribution
9	Identify information that might modify the probabilities specified in step 8
10	If information is free or cheap, buy it (Max SEU)
11	If information costs, find out how much
12	Determine the conditional gain from information purchase

---

*W. Edwards and B. Fasolo. 2001. "Decision technology," *Annual review of psychology* 52: 581–606. Reprinted with permission from CPP, Inc.

13	Aggregate cost of information and gain from having it (Max SEU)
14	Decide whether to buy the information and gain from having it (Max SEU+ Bayes)
15	If information is bought, update prior probabilities (Bayes)
16	Back to Step 11. Iterate till no new information is bought (Max SEU)
17	Assemble the numbers output at steps 6 and 15.
18	Calculate expected utilities (Max SEU)
19	Choose the option with the highest expected utility (Max SEU)

Three interesting points surface from their presentation. First is the role of the Internet and information technology in reducing the costs of gaining more information, leading to the opportunity for making better decisions. (See Step 10.) Second, their model describes a process that is too deliberate and time-consuming for most of the decisions we must make.

Lastly, the conversion of multiple attributes to numbers can be a great challenge, and as previously mentioned, people are not particularly adept at weighting factors. For example, how should I weigh car safety against color, style, or cost? The WPF provides important insights into the multi-attribution decisions that we make about our careers, and organizations must respond to the various factors by adjusting the benefits they provide in order to retain staff, such as providing daycare services to accommodate people trying simultaneously to advance their careers and raise families. While the decision-making process described by Edwards and Fasolo may not be appropriate for every decisions we make, it might be valuable for long-range, strategic planning.

Intellectual impacts of an event can be highly structured and time-consuming, or they can be almost instantaneous. Still, it is the intellectual impact that helps us learn from our mistakes, anticipate future events more fully, take strategic steps to avoid negative outcomes, and maximize positive ones.

One important strategy used by the intellect is to forego immediate pleasures or rewards to obtain more important, more fulfilling, or longer-lasting benefits. This strategy is also used to avoid negative consequences such as an unwanted pregnancy or incarceration from committing a crime. Still, our intellect can never replace our emotions. It is through our emotions that we find love, experience affection and all the related joys from being with other people, and enjoy our successes. It is through our emotions that we experience well-being in terms of happiness, comfort, and sense of involvement, and feel the satisfaction from a life well-lived. The story of Scrooge rings true throughout the ages. Our intellect can apply strategies to obtain wealth, but only through emotional involvement can we experience the complete life.

HUMAN RESOURCE PROGRAMS TO ADDRESS IMPACTS

Organizational health programs and organizational growth and development programs are the HR programs that address work culture, work climate, worker well-being, and intellectual growth.

Organizational Health Programs

Organizational health programs build worker affiliation and trust through a strong work climate and work culture, establishing standards of conduct and promoting effective work behaviors. Organizational health programs also include healthy living programs that build worker physical capacity and well-being. HR managers are often charged with carrying out or overseeing these activities, including training programs to help workers care for themselves, their families, and their coworkers. Many of these programs are presented as employee benefits, which we identify in the WPF as outcomes. Employee assistance programs are designed to help employees deal with short-term but intense problems that affect their health and work performance.

Organizational Growth and Development Programs

The goal of organizational growth and development is to address intellectual impacts and improve reasoning and decision-making at both the organizational and individual levels. To do this, the organization must understand all aspects of work performance as presented in the WPF and strategically address every area.

Strategic planning is at the heart of organizational growth and development. Part of strategic planning includes identifying core organizational values and a desired work culture. While organizations spend a great deal of time in listing their core values, they fail to recognize the entire landscape of values and the methods for institutionalizing these values. In the end, the organization's list of values is often short and coherent, but incomplete.

This shortcoming is due, in part, to a failure to understand the distinction between instrumental values that go into building a strong work climate and terminal values that go into building a strong work culture. The underlying purposes of strategic planning are to think smart and act smart by identifying organizational objectives, setting goals, and directing resources toward achieving those goals.

Organizational growth and development goes beyond the jurisdiction of the HR manager. Still, the HR manager needs to view his own programs as contributing to overall organizational growth and development. For the HR manager, the strategic objectives that directly relate to organizational growth and development are building HR capacity, building performance, and building community.

Previous chapters addressed the evaluation and measurement of service efficiency, and the evaluation and measurement of program benefits and effectiveness. This chapter has discussed programs for building a meaningful work culture and a coherent work climate in order to establish a strong community of workers who understand work performance issues and make good decisions.

A tool for measuring and evaluating work culture and climate is the employee opinion survey, which elicits whether workers understand the key values of the organization, the desired work culture and climate, and the performance expectations that will achieve the organization's goals. The employee opinion survey can also provide feedback on health issues and adversities workers are experiencing that affect their well-being and physical capacity, which leads to the topic of key performance measures.

KEY PERFORMANCE MEASURE—THE EMPLOYEE OPINION SURVEY

The employee opinion survey (EOS) is a useful tool for understanding the thoughts, concerns, and interests of the workers. While people who conduct surveys try to elicit responses from a random sample of the population they are studying, rarely are the respondents truly random because there is a bias created from the willingness of respondents to answer the survey and the availability of the entire population to respond. While the randomness of respondents to employee opinion surveys is probably not affected by the lack of availability, it is definitely affected by the willingness of employees to participate. While an organization might mandate that all employees respond to the survey, many workers are likely to be untruthful, mostly because of concerns over confidentiality.

If the survey is random, it can still be difficult to give meaning to the responses. The measures for validity and reliability are perhaps less important or useful than some suggest. This is not to say that reliability and validity coefficients should not be generated. It simply means that one should be cautious in explaining their meaning. Validity coefficients are based on the respondents being a representative sample of the population and their level of honesty being high. But the better the representation through mandatory participation, the less likely the population will be honest. Reliability coefficients can be raised simply by asking more questions, but the more questions asked, the less likely people will be to voluntarily complete the questionnaire.

If we cannot rely on validity and reliability to extract meaning from the survey, what indicators should we look at? One indicator is the difference in responses from different populations in the organization based on location (division, bureau, worksite), gender, ethnicity, age, job title, and salary grade. Other valuable indicators might include new information or changes in survey results over time.

New Information and Changes in Survey Results

New information can be gained from exploratory, open-ended questions, such as, "What risks are on the horizon that should give this organization concern?" An employee might suggest a new procedure or a change in existing procedures, an opportunity to attract a new customer or constituent, or a new risk on the horizon.

Multiple-choice, scaled responses provide quantifiable results (e.g., on a scale of 1–5 or on a scale ranging from "strongly disagree" to "strongly agree"). Responses might be the same from one holding to the next, telling the organization that its glowing results have been sustained, or its average and poor results have not improved. Changes in survey responses over time tell the organization that the poor results have improved, or that the glowing results have perhaps lost ground or even become better.

Following an intervention implemented by the organization, such as a telecommuting program that allows certain workers to work at home or another remote location, these results can reveal whether work performance and the work community improved, stayed the same, or worsened. Open-ended questions can be linked to multiple-choice questions by asking, "Please explain your response." This presents the opportunity for the respondent to provide information about changes from new initiatives, including unanticipated benefits and unintended consequences.

Interpreting the Results

When the results provide new information or different results, the organization must evaluate the information and decide what action to take, if any. Since new information can be diverse, each suggestion must be viewed on its own merits. Typically, most suggestions are not new information and have already been considered. Still, there will be times when new ideas come forth, and these can be springboards for improvements.

Quantified results can reveal patterns that might be helpful for determining action. When surveys are completed on a voluntary basis, most respondents will have a special interest in the questions. For example, some people will respond because they want to raise a complaint or concern about the issue being surveyed. Other respondents may simply want to voice their support for a job well done.

Even when all workers are required to complete a survey, some questions will have more favorable responses than others. The ratio of positive to negative responses can provide valuable information. For example, if the most common response rate is four positive to one negative, then a positive-response rate of five positive to one negative (or greater) might suggest the organization is performing very well in that area. Conversely, when the positive-to-negative response rate is two positive to one negative (or less), management should review the issue and react accordingly. Having follow-up, open-ended questions allows management to identify underlying problems and make adjustments.

Using Employee Opinion Surveys

The EOS is used to ascertain feedback in areas such as (1) job satisfaction and rewards, including salaries and benefits, doing meaningful work, and having the authority to act; (2) management performance, including management direction, supervisory guidance, and access to resources; and (3) organizational performance, including program accomplishments, work culture and climate, and communication.

By applying the WPF, there are significant opportunities to enhance the EOS with questions that have perhaps been overlooked and use the survey to explain to staff aspects of organizational performance that they may not be fully aware of. Some areas that could be better addressed in employee opinion surveys include the adequacy of staff size, mental abilities, and personalities; levels of effort related to individual initiative and perseverance; access to and effective use of power as an input to performance; opportunities for work improvements and innovations; adversities within the organization that harm performance, along with suggestions to reduce the adversities or prepare workers to deal with them more effectively; and staff well-being and vitality.

Along with the opportunity to expand the survey contents is the opportunity to provide background on the reasons for asking the questions and various issues related to work performance. Topics might include how changes in business processes and technology have led to dramatic increases in productivity through improvements and innovations; issues related to ethics and fairness, including the social contract and its relationship to organizational citizenship; work involvement and comfort as aspects of well-being; and the emotional impacts of empathy, pleasure, and achievement, including the powerful impact that feelings of failure have on both staff and the organization.

Based on the concept of procedural fairness, survey results and actions need to be reported back to people who took the time to complete the surveys. This is especially true when the survey discloses important findings. For example, if the ratio of positive to negative responses is only 2 to 1 regarding supervisory performance, these findings must be shared with the workers, and a strategy established to address the various complaints. Otherwise, the questions should not be asked because the survey will lose its value over time.

THE FUTURE STATE OF HUMAN RESOURCE MANAGEMENT AND RESEARCH OPPORTUNITIES

The part of the WPF that addresses impacts will lead, it is hoped, to a better understanding of organizational culture and climate, and help organizations refine their key values and feedback devices, including the employee opinion survey. In turn, this should lead to improved employee morale and well-being. While one effectiveness measure is to increase employee-job fit, it is not possible to create only desirable jobs or to pay everyone what he would like or feels he needs. Thus the objective of building community is obtained by setting goals to increase present standards and improve work conditions.

There is substantial concern that today's jobs will not be around tomorrow or that tomorrow's jobs will require totally different competencies, so any hope for future employment must be cloaked with guarded optimism. Still, the WPF allows for greater transparency, so workers can gain a better understanding of the employment picture and better prepare themselves for tomorrow's workplace.

This chapter has raised a number of research opportunities. First, although the chapter explored the differences between terminal and instrumental values as developed by Rokeach and how they relate to affiliation and trust, it has not explored which values are perhaps the most critical. Second, while the chapter presented an explanation of impacts, it has not confirmed these hypotheses through experimentation. The WPF's explanation of well-being offers significant opportunities for research and investigation. One line of research is the role that involvement plays in vitality and organizational citizenship.

Another opportunity is the relationship between well-being and adversities. Research might explore the effects of interventions on individual well-being and work performance, as well as the effects of reducing or eliminating adversities. Another area of research is testing the WPF's proposition that attitudes are more accessible but less refined and reliable than intellectual judgments. At the macro level, there are enormous opportunities to investigate, test, and explain the differences between the cause-effect relationship with inputs, processes, and outputs and the action-reaction relationship between outputs, outcomes, and impacts.

WHAT MAKES A GOOD WORKER?

At the conclusion of Part 3, we again return to the question of what makes a good worker—this time from the perspective of outcomes and impacts. A good worker provides services that are beneficial to society. He manages risks associated with new initiatives to limit or avoid unintended consequences, and he is willing to take on adversities and greater obligations in pursuit of advancement and career success. He evaluates his own performance and the performance of others, and he recognizes their accomplishments and rewards them for their contributions. He ensures that workers, customers, and other stakeholders are treated fairly and given explanations for actions, and that they are given a voice to dissent or appeal.

At the impact level, the good worker shares the terminal and instrumental values of the organization and adds to the work culture and climate by pursuing important accomplishments and building trust and affiliation with others. The good worker reveals vitality by being positive and cheerful, comfortable in his role, and highly involved in the organization's work. He understands the values, hopes, and aspirations of other people and strives to make their lives better, while holding them accountable for their work activities and behaviors. Finally, the good worker is revealed through his understanding, beliefs, judgments, and decisions that add to organizational capacity, performance, and community.

This chapter differentiated impacts from outcomes and showed how psychology plays an integral part in understanding impacts or the reactions of workers to work outputs and outcomes. It distinguished terminal values related to emotional impacts from instrumental values associated with psychological judgments and attitudes. It showed how the intellect plays a unique role in helping us to understand our attitudes, emotions, and the world we live in. Through this understanding we are able to make better decisions and improve our lives and our organizations.

Building a Human Resource Performance Dashboard

T his final chapter begins by summarizing the Work Performance Framework (WPF) using the information and ideas contained in the rest of the book. Next, the chapter presents a performance dashboard as a tool for HR strategic planning and program evaluation to show how the HR manager can use the WPF in practice to develop a strategic HR plan and make effective program decisions.

The chapter then addresses the question of what makes a good worker, exploring the question from the perspective of the organization, applying the lessons learned from this book, and contemplating what the good worker will be in the future. It also addresses what makes a good worker from the workers' perspective, to help them understand the present and future work environment and what they can do to increase their value to the organization. The chapter concludes by summarizing critical issues in the field of HR management developed or referenced in this book that are ripe for future research.

THE WORK PERFORMANCE FRAMEWORK

Five-sixths of the workers in our economy work in the service-providing industries, while the goods-producing industries employ the other sixth. The vast majority of workers in the public sector are in the service-providing industry, so the focus of this book is on services rather than goods as work outputs, and worker productivity is measured in terms of efficiency and effectiveness.

The primary measure of service efficiency is cost per unit of service, or cost per output, while secondary measures include:

- Intake, or the number of requests for services

- Production, or the number of units of service provided

- Backlog, or the number of requests for services not yet completed

- Completion rate, or the percentage of service requests that ultimately are completed or are completed without errors

- Average cycle time, or the average time it takes to complete a service

- Service timeliness, or the percentage of services completed by a deadline, as in the case of payroll services, which must be completed every pay period

- Access, or number of people who access the services or related information and the speed of access.

Effectiveness measures evaluate work outcomes and impacts. Effectiveness measures for work outcomes address:

- Program benefits

- Unintended consequences

- Worker rewards and punishments

- New obligations and adversities for workers

- Performance measures to evaluate work performance and results

- Fairness to stakeholders (e.g., program recipients, workers, taxpayers, political leaders, interest groups).

Effectiveness measures for impacts address:

- Affiliation tied to emotions and terminal values (e.g., security, pleasure, human relations, achievement)

- Trust tied to attitudes and instrumental values (e.g., virtues, ethics, and fairness)

- Well-being, or vitality based on happiness, comfort, and involvement

- Beliefs and decision-making based on intellectual assessments of effectiveness, efficiency, and reliability.

For the HR manager, HR service-effectiveness measures evaluate his or her contributions to the organization in managing the workforce and managing the workplace through building HR capacity, performance, and community. Building HR capacity means:

- Establishing and classifying needed positions

- Acquiring and keeping people with needed talents and abilities

- Establishing and using enabling programs that transform these talents and abilities into the knowledge, skills, and abilities (KSAs) needed to complete work.

Building HR performance means:

- Increasing worker's inputs in carrying out work responsibilities by increasing their applied KSAs, effort, and power as they perform work

- Improving work processes in the areas of production, behaviors, and improvements/innovations

- Improving outputs or program services, improving interpersonal communication, and building better work systems.

Building HR community means:

- Recognizing and rewarding workers for their work performance

- Helping workers handle adversities

- Building affiliation by addressing workers' emotional needs and aspirations tied to terminal values involving security, pleasure, human relations, and achievement

- Building trust in the organization by addressing workers' attitudes and judgments tied to instrumental values involving fairness, ethics, and virtues

- Building workers' well-being and vitality derived from happiness, comfort, and involvement

- Building workers' intellectual understanding of the organization and decision-making by providing them important information about the organization (with the WPF as a guide).

STRATEGIC HUMAN RESOURCE MANAGEMENT

Strategic HR management means managing with the desired end-state in mind. The WPF provides a framework for the HR manager to use to pursue the strategic objectives of building HR capacity, building performance, and building community, thus laying the foundation for the strategic management of the organization. Four ways to achieve these objectives are to:

1. Evaluate HR work processes and make key business-process improvements.

2. Measure the efficiency of key HR services and increase efficiency.

3. Evaluate customer reaction to HR services and make key improvements to increase effectiveness and satisfaction.

4. Determine baseline performance and industry standards; first achieve and then surpass industry standards.

Regardless of the service being provided, certain processes must be completed in support of the services:

- Provide forms, information, consultations, training, and reviews.
- Record service activities.
- Notify stakeholders.
- Obtain stakeholder feedback.
- Track and analyze data.
- Make policy and process improvements.
- Report on service activities and initiatives.

For example, an HR manager might decide to implement a healthy day initiative to increase worker awareness of good health. The service might include a series of training programs and activities. For people to attend, they must fill out a form. They might want information on the programs being offered and have questions that need to be answered. If the program becomes adopted permanently, it might be included as a part of new employee orientation (training). There might also be certain requirements to participate (review).

Records need to be maintained on who is approved to participate and who participated, and participants must be notified of their inclusion in the event and successful completion of the program. A survey instrument might be used to determine the reaction of participants and the organization's managers. Do the workers and managers believe the program contributed to the overall well-being of staff, or was it a waste of time?

The participation rate, reactions, and change in workers' performance and well-being can be tracked and analyzed to evaluate the program's benefits and identify opportunities to make the program better. With this information, policies and procedures can be revised.

Finally, the activities must be reported to management as a part of the HR manager's overall workload and contribution to the organization. Information reported might include participation rate, benefits, aggregated information on the responses to the program, and the progress of initiatives to improve the program. All of these steps might not be followed for every HR program, but the HR manager needs to look at the HR services and decide whether they should be.

Process improvements involving these steps might include:

- Using the intranet as a resource for forms, general information, answers to frequently asked questions (FAQs), taped training modules, and contact information for various HR programs and services

- Refining record-keeping and documentation to make them more useful for tracking information, analyzing data, and evaluating the effectiveness and efficiency of policy and process improvements

- Increasing the use of surveys and feedback loops on service effectiveness and stakeholder satisfaction

- Developing policy and process improvements based on data analyses and stakeholder feedback

- Providing informative reports on HR activities, initiatives, and successes that are tied to service and strategic objectives.

With the correct processes in place, the HR manager can then evaluate service effectiveness and efficiency. Baseline information is derived from measurements of past performance. For example, the HR manager can use the annual averages for the time it took to fill a position over the last three years as the baseline measure for evaluating the likely average time for the current year. If the HR manager has introduced new policies or procedures, the goal would be to set a target of a shorter average time.

In the public service HR management community there is great interest in devising industry standards for HR services. At present these standards do not exist. HR professional associations are working on benchmarks, best practices, and measures being tracked by organizations willing to respond to their surveys. For example, IPMA-HR has recently established its Benchmarking Committee, whose charge is to conduct benchmarking surveys and suggest best practices. Without industry standards or benchmarks, the HR manager's best alternative is to use baseline measures and seek to continuously improve the performance of key services.

A DASHBOARD FOR REPORTING HUMAN RESOURCE PROGRAM PERFORMANCE

A dashboard is a brief report, usually one page, for managing program performance. Table 9-1 presents strategic HR objectives aligned with HR service objectives, HR goals, efficiency and effectiveness indicators, and policy and process initiatives. To give the reader a quick understanding of the dashboard, a legend can be used to color the various cells indicating whether the performance in that area is good, marginal, or poor.

The top of the dashboard lists the three strategic objectives for the HR manager:

- Building HR capacity
- Building HR performance
- Building HR community.

TABLE 9-1 A Human Resources Performance Dashboard

Strategic Objectives	Building HR Capacity	Building HR Performance	Building HR Community
Service Objectives	Manage Staffing the Agency; Manage Staff Development	Manage Staff Performance; Manage Diversity, Fairness, and Legal Compliance	Manage Rewards and Benefits; Manage the Work Environment
Goals	Higher Staff Capacity	Higher Staff Performance; Legal Compliance and Greater Diversity	Higher Employee Work Satisfaction and Well-Being; Richer Work Culture and Work Climate
Effectiveness Indicators	HR Capacity Survey	Work Performance Reports; HR Performance Survey; HR Services Performance Survey	Employee Opinion Survey; New Employee Survey; Exit Survey
Efficiency Indicators	See below	See below	See below
Policy and Process Initiatives	Improvements; Innovations	Improvements; Innovations	Improvements; Innovations

Strategic Objective	HR Services Inventory	Efficiency Measures
Building HR Capacity	Classification Inventory	# of Classified Positions, Organizational Chart
	Classification	# of Classification Requests, # of Completed Classifications, Backlog, Cycle Time, Completion Rate
	Staffing Inventory	# of Positions Filled, # of Vacant Positions, Approved Fill Levels
	Appointments/Promotions	Fill Requests, Appointments, Backlog, Cycle Time
	Examinations	# of Examination Requests, # of Examinations, Backlog, Cycle Time, Completion Rate
	Decentralized Examinations	# of Candidates Tested
	Recruitment	# of Recruitment Activities, # of Contacts, # of Applicants, # of Appointments
	Retention	Retention Rate
	Training and Development Inventory	# of Staff Trained, # of Staff with Training Needs
	Training and Development	# of Training Requests, # of Completed Sessions, Backlog, # of Participants, Participation Rate
	Traineeships	# of Traineeships, Successful Completion Rate

Building HR Performance	Performance Inventory	Staff Performance Level
	Performance Management	# of Service Requests, # of Completed Services, Backlog, Participation Rate
	Performance Evaluation	Completion Rate of Documentation, Timeliness, Accuracy, Aggregate Ratings
	Probation Evaluation	Completion Rate of Documentation, Timeliness, Accuracy, Successful Completion Rate
	Attendance	Attendance Rate
	Employee History Records	# of Records, Usage
	Employee Relations	# of Disciplinary Cases and Grievances, # of Appeals, Success Rate
	Diversity	Rate of Diversity
	Personnel Transactions	# of Transactions Completed, Timeliness, Accuracy
Building HR Community	Employee Satisfaction Inventory	Employee Satisfaction Levels
	Payroll Services	# of Employees Paid, Timeliness, Accuracy
	Time and Attendance	# of Timesheets, Timeliness, Accuracy
	Employee Benefits	# of Claims, # of Assists
	Leaves and Separations	# of Leaves and Separations, # of Assists
	Retirement	# of Retirements, # of Assists
	Workers Compensation	# of Claims, # of Assists
	Employee Recognition	# of Participants
	Organizational Health	# of Service Requests, # of Completed Services, Backlog, Participation Rate
	Health Services	# of Service Requests, # of Completed Services, Backlog, Participation Rate
	Employee Assistance Program	# of Service Requests, # of Completed Services, Backlog, Participation Rate

If the HR manager focuses on these three objectives, and is successful in achieving them, she is doing a good job.

Next, six service objectives that are tied to the three strategic objectives are listed:

- Manage staffing the agency (building HR capacity)
- Manage staff development (building HR capacity)
- Manage staff performance (building HR performance)
- Manage diversity, fairness, and legal compliance (building HR performance)
- Manage rewards and benefits (building HR community)
- Manage the work environment (building HR community).

Table 9-1 then identifies HR goals in terms of the strategic and service objectives:

- Higher staff capacity (building HR capacity and related service objectives)
- Higher staff performance (building HR performance and related service objectives)
- Legal compliance and greater diversity (building HR performance and related service objectives)
- Higher employee work satisfaction and well-being (building HR community and related service objectives)
- Richer work climate and work culture (building HR community and related service objectives).

Effectiveness indicators are at the next level. While surveys are presented in the dashboard as the primary source of information on effectiveness, other indicators can be acquired from experts or customer focus groups or, as mentioned, industry standards or benchmarks, where available.

Efficiency indicators listed at the top of the dashboard are a composite assessment of the discrete efficiency measures aligned with strategic objectives and services found in the bottom section of the dashboard. For example, classification is listed as a service that addresses the strategic objective of building capacity. The first measure is a classification inventory of the number of classified positions, and an organizational chart to see where they exist. The efficiency measures for classification services are:

- Number of classification requests (intake)
- Number of completed requests (work production)
- Backlog
- Cycle time
- Completion rate.

Breakdowns for divisions and bureaus can identify whether some parts of the organization are better served than others, or contribute to unfavorable measures. For example, one division might be submitting classification requests that have a high cycle time and a low completion rate. Upon further investigation, the HR manager might find that the supporting documentation is incomplete, erroneous, or unrealistic.

Finally, policy and process initiatives that are intended to serve as improvements or innovations are presented. These initiatives are aligned with strategic objectives, service objectives, goals, effectiveness measures, and efficiency measures. This allows the HR manager to project strategic-level improvements in concert with efficiency and effectiveness measures. Using this classification example, the HR manager can develop training material to help the problem division improve the quality of its classification requests and refrain from submitting requests that will likely be disapproved. This will result in improved classification services and ultimately help build capacity by decreasing the cycle time for critical classification requests.

While recording service information and tracking and analyzing data might be somewhat challenging, the dashboard provides the HR manager with a number of efficiency measures to look at. She might choose to develop measures for all those identified or concentrate on just a few. For example, she might want to evaluate her staffing program based on a few key measures related to classification, appointments and promotions, and retention. Key measures might include:

- The number of positions classified, the number of classification requests completed, and the average cycle time

- The number of positions filled and the number of appointments and promotions

- The employee retention rate.

While not appearing on the dashboard, more detailed information should also be tracked. Appointments and retention might be broken down by division to see which divisions are struggling to retain staff, or by title to see which titles might require better recruitment and selection.

Once the HR manager decides on the measures to be taken, she must determine what platform to use for recording the information. Any desktop computer has the memory capacity to maintain the HR records, and statistical software can be purchased to generate statistics not easily calculated by Excel software. However, off-line computerization may be more cumbersome than imbedding the records, record maintenance, and reports into the central computer system. With centralized record-keeping, standard reports can be generated and made available upon demand for the organizational leaders and program managers.

Formal surveys are being used more extensively because they provide important information on service effectiveness. Various survey software packages and instruments are available, and some of these can make creating a survey and generating reports rather easy. The HR manager must first decide what effectiveness information is needed. Returning to the strategic objectives of building capacity, building performance, and building community, a straightforward method is to simply ask the program managers these questions:

- Do you have the staff you need?

- Do you have the positions you need?

- Are your workers getting the training they need?

- Are you able to retain your highly productive workers?

- Are you able to improve the performance of your low producers?

- Are you able to terminate poorly performing workers?

- Are your workers satisfied with their work?

- Are your workers satisfied with their work environment?

- Are your workers able to balance work life and home life demands?

Unfortunately, the program managers may not know the answers to these questions or want to address personnel problems. Surveys with greater depth or involving broader groups of respondents, including customers and other stakeholders, might provide different answers and reveal problems or improvement opportunities.

The WPF can be useful in delving into many meaningful questions. To build capacity, questions about staff's initial abilities might address whether they have the talent, aptitude, or creativity to take on new assignments, the personality traits to work well with others, and the analytical abilities to analyze and solve problems. Questions about enabling pro-grams might address whether they sufficiently prepare workers to carry out normal work production, follow correct work behaviors, and conduct process improvements.

To build performance, questions about staff inputs might ask if the staff is applying the required KSAs, demonstrating high effort, using authority and resources effectively, and demonstrating the ability to gain the cooperation of other workers. Other questions related to the WPF can be developed to address work processes, work outputs, work outcomes, and work impacts. The critical point to remember is that the questions should provide some insight into the organization's ability to evaluate whether the HR programs and services are helping to achieve the strategic objectives of building HR capacity, building performance, and building community.

One area missing on the dashboard is costs. As has been discussed, cost per unit of service is the most important efficiency measure. Return on investment (ROI) in human resources is becoming recognized as a criti-cal part of program planning and management. Once HR performance measures are in place, the HR manager can work with the finance office to develop links between HR costs and performance. But there are many steps to be taken to evaluate the effectiveness and efficiency of HR services before evaluating ROI.

Although the dashboard in Table 9-1 is helpful for the HR manager in managing her HR programs, it may be too much information to serve as a dashboard for reporting to higher management. A streamlined ver-sion will likely be needed. Table 9-2 provides an abbreviated version that includes the strategic and service objectives only.

TABLE 9-2 Human Resources Reporting Dashboard		
Strategic Objectives	1) Building HR Capacity	2) Building HR Performance	3) Building HR Community
Service Objectives	1a) Manage Staffing the Agency	2a) Manage Staff Performance	3a) Manage Rewards and Benefits
	1b) Manage Staff Development	2b) Manage Diversity, Fairness, and Legal Compliance	3b) Manage the Work Environment

The abbreviated dashboard will be easy for the agency leader to understand. Color codes (e.g., red = alert, yellow = caution, green = solid performance) can be used to identify performance levels for each section of the dashboard, and the HR manager can provide supporting performance measures upon request.

WHAT MAKES A GOOD WORKER?

At the conclusion of Part 1, it was proposed that general mental abilities and certain personality traits can increase the likelihood of a new worker's becoming a valued employee. A person who is continuously interested in gaining new skills, learning new information, networking with people inside and outside the organization, and becoming more technologically proficient is likely to be more successful in the new work environment. And a person who helps others to learn will be a treasured asset.

At the end of Part 2, the good worker was described as someone who applies the needed competencies to her work, demonstrates high effort, understands the role of power, and uses her power effectively. The good worker is productive, uses appropriate work behaviors to develop trust and affiliation, and understands and uses the tools for continuous improvement to increase her own productivity and that of her organization. Finally, the good worker provides efficient services, communicates her work and aspirations with others, listens to and understands the aspirations of other workers, and helps to build better work systems and services.

At the end of Part 3, it was proposed that at the outcome level a good worker provides services that are beneficial to society, manages risks associated with new initiatives to limit or avoid unintended consequences, is willing to take on adversities and greater obligations in pursuit of career advancement, evaluates her performance and the performance of others, recognizes the accomplishments of other people and rewards them for their contributions, and ensures that workers, customers, and other stakeholders are treated fairly, presented with explanations for actions, and given a voice to dissent.

At the impact level, a good worker shares the terminal and instrumental values of the organization and adds to the work culture and climate by seeking important accomplishments and building trust and affiliation with others. The good worker reveals vitality by being positive and cheerful, and is comfortable in her role and highly involved in the organization's work. She understands the values, hopes, and aspirations of other people and strives to make their lives better, while holding them accountable for their work activities and behaviors. Finally, the good worker is revealed through her understanding, beliefs, judgments, and decisions that add to organizational capacity, performance, and community.

The Future Public-Sector Organization

What will the future public-sector organization look like? First, organizations now freely question whether work needs to be done in-house or if it can be accomplished by using outside contractors. These questions are not limited to the work associated with computers. Extensive contracting of services has raised concerns that there will be relatively few public servants left, and their main responsibilities will be limited to pass-through activities of collecting and distributing funds and monitoring the work of private-sector and nonprofit contractors. These concerns have led to the charge that public administration is becoming a "hollow state."

Second, temporary workers are now regularly used in public programs. While the installation of computer systems was first seen as a temporary activity to be performed by highly technical outside vendors, computer and telecommunications systems conversions, upgrades, and in-house improvements are now seen as continuous work. This experience has led to a fuzzy distinction between what is permanent work and what is temporary work, as well as who is a permanent worker and who is a temporary worker.

While the concept of continuous improvement suggests ongoing activities, these activities are often perceived as a series of temporary projects. Because of tight timelines and competing work priorities, workers on temporary computer projects have become skilled at estimating and tracking workload, reinforcing the concept of work as a series of temporary assignments. From a cost-cutting perspective, temporary workers are desirable because they are perceived as less expensive due to lower benefits, and their jobs are more easily eliminated when a project ends.

A private-sector organization wants the best worker for the least cost, and it will pay more for workers whose abilities are in high demand and short supply. With a global marketplace for recruiting, a large private-sector firm has an enormous supply of workers with diverse abilities to draw from, including a large population of immigrants who have entered the United States in recent years.

The public sector has two primary objectives: providing the many critical services that are not practical for private industry to provide and promoting social justice. While public agencies want the skilled workers that are in high demand and short supply, to maintain a stable society the agencies must also address the needs of people who want a decent job and a good life. While private industry provides stiff competition with the public sector in purchasing the scarce human resources, they are driving down the value of the less-skilled worker by drawing from the global marketplace. Although the impending transition of the baby boom generation into retirement could perhaps provide a stabilizing effect on the employment market for the average worker, particularly since there will be increased service needs for the elderly population, the global workforce may be recruited to provide many of these services to keep costs down.

The public sector will have a difficult time competing with the private sector for top talent, but is likely to be called upon to prop up the value of the less-skilled worker. Thus building HR capacity, building performance, and building community are not only strategic objectives for the HR manager but also critical for all of public service and for our society as a whole.

What the Worker Needs to Know

The employment market is much more selective than a generation ago. This trend is likely to continue. As measurements of market conditions have provided insights into product and service quality improvements, so too have measurements and studies of employment markets led to more sophisticated selection processes for hiring new workers. This has led to a narrowing of opportunities for good-paying jobs. While the highly skilled worker will benefit disproportionately in this new work environment, the unskilled and under-skilled worker will disproportionately suffer. In this new world, what does the worker need to know?

Start Early

People who fail to understand and prepare for the new work environment early on in their lives will be at a distinct disadvantage. Parents need to prepare their children for the new work environment, and young people need to use school and extra-curricular activities to understand the employer's point of view. A young worker must be better prepared than the other job candidates by taking advantage, early and often, of opportunities to develop her skills and talents, refine those behaviors valued in the workplace, and learn from real-life work experiences.

Specialize

Choose a field of study; identify trends and future specialty areas; and specialize in one or several of these areas. While job-person fit is very important to long-term happiness, be sure the specialty area you choose provides real employment opportunities. If there is low demand or a high supply of specialists for the special field you are considering, you will be less likely to succeed in pursuing your dreams. In New York State, the supply of elementary school teachers is very high, and new graduates have difficulty finding jobs. Conversely, high school science and mathematics teachers are in much greater demand because of low supply. Some very popular specialty workers, like actors and musicians, are underpaid because more than enough people are interested in the work.

Learn Technologies

Knowledge of computer and telecommunication technology multiplies the value of a worker's skills. An auditor uses auditing software; an engineer uses engineering software; and a graphics artist uses graphic arts software. The Internet expands communication from one person to millions; get to know all that it can do. Even though many people are not comfortable with computer programming, it is important to understand how programming works and what computerization can do to enhance your special skills in order to prepare for employment in the future work environment.

Understand the Value of Good Work Behaviors and Learn Related Competencies

First, understand the importance of building affiliation and trust, and then learn and practice behaviors that generate appropriate interpersonal communication. Keep in mind that the art of interpersonal communication is not simply communicating your own values but also understanding and connecting with the other person and her values. Make sure you are seen as a member of the work team in good standing.

Be Creative

Learn your field of work and your specialty area so well that you can identify new opportunities for growth and improvement or areas that are underdeveloped. Learn how to take a thought for a new or improved product or service to its final form. Recognize that you do not need to do it all, but you must understand the steps for improvements and innovations, your role in the process, and the resources you will need, including human resources.

Work Hard

Put in the time and effort. Understand that part of effort is intention, so commit yourself to the various levels of intention—self-discipline, self-efficacy, willingness, initiative, and perseverance. Increase your energy level to sustain yourself when your work and home demands increase. You will be expected to work long hours and continuously learn new information and skills. Learn how to gain power and use it effectively by getting (or sometimes assuming) the authority to act, acquiring needed resources and using them efficiently, and influencing others to be active, productive participants.

The foregoing may not be a complete list of what a worker needs to know in the new work environment. Can one succeed without doing all these things? Perhaps. The essential thing to remember is that in the new work environment we are evaluated on how we approach opportunities in life. We are expected to actively pursue opportunities for our own growth and development, and to help others along the way. The new organization is extremely wary of the worker who will sabotage her career or the work of her coworkers. What you do not know about yourself can hurt you, so pursue self-awareness at all times.

The Internet has become a place where antisocial words and behaviors are rampant. Many people believe they can say things online that they wouldn't say face-to-face or post activities that they wouldn't participate in when being watched. But in reality, they are acting in a public forum, and these activities can result in long-term damage to their reputations. The level of transparency and public exposure on the Internet will very likely carry over to the future workplace, and the worker must recognize that she is a much more public figure than ever before.

THE FUTURE STATE OF HUMAN RESOURCE MANAGEMENT AND RESEARCH OPPORTUNITIES

The WPF can be used in conjunction with the three strategic objectives of building HR capacity, building performance, and building community to identify important HR management issues for future research.

Building Human Resource Capacity

Building HR capacity involves bringing in key human resources from outside the organization, retaining them, and, once on board, enabling them to perform work duties and activities. The WPF presents human resources (general mental abilities, physical abilities, and socioeconomic conditions) and enablers (training/education, experience, healthy activities, and special assistance) as antecedents to the general systems theory components of inputs, processes, and outputs. Research opportunities involving antecedents include:

- Explain antecedents and identify additional components not presented in the WPF.

- Apply the categories of antecedents presented in the WPF to research in other social sciences.

For much of the 20th century, personality was seen as essential to the behavioral and leadership aspects of work. Because of the importance of continuous improvement, recent attention has been given to creativity as a human resource. With the increases in productivity through technology in the last several decades, improvements and innovations have become a core work process, even in the public sector.

Research opportunities in the areas of building capacity include:

- Explore what creativity is, who has it, and whether it can be learned through training.

- Explore the future role of technology as a magnifier of capacity, particularly for the average worker seeking to find a job in the new work environment.

- Explore the future role of robots, computers, and telecommunications in the workplace and the meaning (benefits and unintended consequences) to the worker.

- Explore the future role of technology in recruitment and enabling activities to achieve greater service efficiency and effectiveness.

- Explore the various opportunities for becoming enabled, and how people take advantage of or pass over these opportunities.

- Explore the variation between organizations in building their HR capacity.

Building Human Resource Performance

Building HR performance involves monitoring staff inputs, work processes, and work outputs; evaluating performance; and making adjustments to increase work performance and the quality and quantity of outputs (services).

The WPF explains the human resources inputs of competencies (applied abilities), effort, and power as the causes of work performance. Related research opportunities include:

- Develop job performance evaluations based on these three sets of inputs.
- Test causal relationships between these inputs and work performance.

The WPF provides insights into research opportunities related to building HR performance, including:

- Explore the role of effort and power as inputs as presented in the WPF.
- Explore work behaviors as processes rather than inputs and identify behaviors that best establish trust and affiliation in different work settings.
- Explore the variation in work behaviors and methods of establishing trust and affiliation between organizations, including public-sector versus private-sector organizations.
- Explore the work processes of innovations and improvements, including business systems analyses and computerization.
- Explore the relationship between information and services.
- Explore the variation among organizations in building HR performance.

Building Human Resource Community

Building HR community involves evaluating and improving the fairness and effectiveness of program benefits and reducing unintended, unwanted consequences for customers and constituents, as well as improving the fairness and effectiveness of rewards, punishments, future obligations, and adversities for the worker. Building community also involves increasing the beneficial impacts of program services and outcomes on worker and stakeholder affiliation, trust, well-being, and understanding of program operations and services.

The WPF presents outcomes as reactions to work outputs, and impacts as reactions to outputs and outcomes. Related research opportunities include:

- Test the action-reaction relationships in work performance systems.

- Explore the action-reaction relationship in other social sciences.

The WPF presents additional insights into research opportunities for building HR community, including:

- Test the concepts of attitudes, work climate, work culture, and well-being as presented in the WPF.

- Explore variations among organizations in building HR community.

- Explore and test the relationships between HR capacity, performance, and community.

As a part of fairness and social justice, equity and equality are at two ends of a continuum. There is a prime research opportunity to explore the variations in societies based on their positions on this continuum. In the WPF the social contract is the fourth component of fairness and social justice, and it may be one of the more glaring omissions in contemporary research and discussion. There is a research opportunity in linking organizational citizenship to fairness, social justice, and the social contract.

Adversities have not been closely examined as an outcome associated with rewards for appointments and promotions, yet they are perhaps the greatest challenge for newly appointed supervisors, managers, and organizational leaders. Identifying such adversities and how they are best dealt with is yet another prime opportunity for meaningful research in HR.

FUTURE HUMAN RESOURCE MANAGEMENT POLICY ISSUES

For many reasons, the future seems quite tenuous, and certain concerns will surface in the public-sector organization that the HR manager to help resolve. Massive policy issues that will affect the functions and composition of future government employment include security needs to address the dangers of weapons of mass destruction, the continuing growth in the world population, and the challenges of managing the natural environment. Unlike any time in the past, these three issues are so large that they threaten to alter human existence as we know it. These anxieties are sure to be felt in the workplace.

At the next level of policy issues are threats that could destabilize our economy, although not jeopardize our existence. These include high government debt, high health care and Social Security costs as a proportion of the costs of doing business, competition with a global workforce, a shortage of workers for critical jobs, and an abundance of workers for non-critical jobs. The future supply of workers and costs of employee benefits directly concern HR managers.

The increased capacity of organizations to innovate and improve is creating conflicts between work production, work behaviors, and improvements/innovations. Low-skilled jobs are often eliminated when the work can be performed by computers. Other work-production procedures regularly change and require continuous retraining of staff, particularly in the use of new tools of technology. As performance levels improve, production standards are revised and raised. With job security being more tenuous, building trust and affiliation is made more difficult.

Organizations are less tolerant of problem employees and more selective of new workers, and many new workers are more skilled and less committed to their organization because they understand the temporary nature of jobs in the current environment. Unions have also had to adapt to the new environment. Protecting jobs by resisting change is not acceptable in the new work environment. These conditions pose serious challenges for HR professionals to facilitate organizational changes, maintain worker job satisfaction and commitment, and recruit and train staff in new technologies.

Work performance has always been recognized as an important factor in organizational effectiveness. It is also important to workers, even when they do not understand everything involved with building a career. Failure is one of our greatest motivators, and de-motivators. Although many workers understand the importance of their work performance and have received the career guidance they needed along the way, many more workers spend their careers unaware of the mistakes they make or the opportunities they pass over. Some workers work hard to climb the ladder of success and constantly ask themselves, "What do I want in life?" and "What is the probability that this opportunity will help me to reach my goals?" Unfortunately, many workers never get the help they need to understand all that's involved with building a career.

To date there has not been a theoretical framework to organize the many theories, beliefs, and practices on work performance. The WPF can serve as an important start. HR managers can use the WPF to provide clarity and transparency in their organizations so the average workers, like the high performers, understand the importance of that next opportunity and what it takes to perform well.

References

CHAPTER 1

Behn, R.D. 1995. "The big questions of public management," *Public administration review* 55.4: 313–24.

Frederickson, H.G. 1997. *The spirit of public administration.* San Francisco, CA: Jossey-Bass Inc.

Hatry, H.P. 2001. "What types of performance should be tracked?" *Quicker, better, cheaper? Managing performance in American government.* D. Forsythe, ed., 17–34. Albany, NY: The Rockefeller Institute Press.

Jackson, S.E., and R.S. Schuler. 1995. "Understanding human resource management in the context of organizations and their environments," *Annual Review of Psychology* 46: 237–64.

Raadschelders, J.C.N. 1999. "A coherent framework for the study of public administration," *Journal of public administration and research* 9.2: 281–303.

Southworth, D.E. 2001. "A vision for the next century—government without corruption," a paper presented at the 62nd National Conference, American Society for Public Administration, Newark, New Jersey.

Wright, P.M., and S.A. Snell 1991. "Toward an integrative view of strategic human resource management," *Human resource management review* 1: 203–25.

CHAPTER 2

Bandura, A. 2001. "Social cognition theory," *Annual review of psychology* 52: 1–26.

Byham, W.C. "What is an assessment center? The assessment center method, applications, and technologies." Development Dimensions International. Online at http://www.assessmentcenters.org/articles/whatisassess2.asp (accessed November 4, 2008).

Dulewicz, V., and M. Higgs. 2004. "Can emotional intelligence be developed?" *International journal of human resource management* 15.1: 95–111.

The Equal Employment Opportunity Commission. 2008. "Disability Discrimination." The Equal Employment Opportunity Commission. Online at http://www.eeoc.gov/types/ada.html (accessed November 4, 2008).

Fisicaro, S.A., and C.E. Lance. 1990. "Implications of three causal models for the measurement of halo effect," *Applied psychological measurement* 14: 419–29.

Funder, D.C. 2001. "Personality," *Annual review of psychology* 52: 197–221.

Hunter, J.E., and F.L. Schmidt 1990. *Methods of meta-analysis: correcting error and bias in research findings.* Beverly Hills: Sage.

Hunter, J. E., F.L. Schmidt, and M.K. Judiesch. 1990. "Individual differences in output variability as a function of job complexity," *Journal of applied psychology* 75.1: 28–42.

Hunter, J.E., F.L. Schmidt, and G.B. Jackson. 1982. *Meta-analysis: cumulating research findings across studies.* Beverly Hills: Sage. (In Schmidt & Hunter 1998).

Mayer, J.D., and P. Salovey. 1997. "What is emotional intelligence?" *Emotional development and emotional intelligence: implications for educators.* P. Salovey and D. Sluyter, eds., 3–31. New York: Basic Books.

Mischel, W., and Y. Shoda. 1998. "Reconciling processing dynamics and personality dispositions," *Annual review of psychology* 49: 229–58.

Mount, M.K., and M.R. Barrick. 1995. "The big five personality dimensions: Implications for research and practice in human research management," *Research in personnel and human resources management* 13: 153–200.

Murphy, K.R., B.E. Cronin, and A.P. Tam. 2003. "Controversy and consensus regarding the use of cognitive ability testing in organizations," *Journal of Applied Psychology* 88.4: 660–71.

New York State Department of Civil Service. 2006. "Workforce management report." New York State Department of Civil Service. Online at http://www.cs.state.ny.us/hr/docs/2006.pdf (accessed October 5, 2008).

The Philippine Nurses Association of New York. Online at http://www.pnanewyork.org (accessed October 5, 2008).

Salovey, P., and D. Sluyter, eds., 1997. *Emotional development and emotional intelligence: implications for educators.* New York: Basic Books.

Schmidt, F.L., and J.E. Hunter. 1998. "The validity and utility of selection methods in personnel psychology: practical and theoretical implications of 85 years of research findings," *Psychological bulletin* 124.2: 262–74.

Sternberg, R.J., and J.C. Kaufman. 1998. "Human Abilities," *Annual review of psychology* 49: 479–502.

U.S. Office of Personnel Management. "Federal employment statistics—highlights 2004." U.S. Office of Personnel Management. Online at http://www.opm.gov/feddata/retire/rs2004_highlights.pdf (accessed November 4, 2008).

U.S. Office of Personnel Management. "Standards for agency HRM accountability systems under the merit system principles." U.S. Office of Personnel Management. Online at https://www.opm.gov/ACCOUNT/standards.asp (accessed November 4, 2008).

Wilson, M., and W.C. Wang. 1995. "Complex composites: issues that arise in combining different modes of assessment," *Applied psychological measurement* 19: 51–71.

CHAPTER 3

Ammons, D.N., and P.A. Niedzielski-Eichner. 1985. "Evaluating supervisory training in local government: moving beyond concept to a practical framework," *Public personnel management* 14.3: 211–30.

Cannon-Bowers, J.A., and E. Salas, eds. 1998. *Making decisions under stress: Implications for individual and team training.* Washington, D.C.: American Psychological Association.

Driskell, J.E., and J.H. Johnston. 1998. "Stress exposure training," *Making decisions under stress: implications for individual and team training.* J.A. Cannon-Bowers and E. Salas, eds., 191–217. Washington, D.C.: American Psychological Association.

Johnston, J.H., and J.A. Cannon-Bowers. 1996. "Training for stress exposure," *Stress and human performance.* J.E. Driskel and E. Salas, eds., 223–56. Mahweh, NJ: Erlbaum.

Salas, E., and J.A. Cannon-Bowers. 2001. "The science of training: a decade of progress," *Annual review of psychology* 52: 471–99.

CHAPTER 4

Baum, J.R., and E.A. Locke. 2004. "The relationship of entrepreneurial traits, skills, and motivation to subsequent ventures," *Journal of applied psychology* 89: 587–99.

Bollen, K.A. 2002. "Latent variables in psychology and the social sciences," *Annual review of psychology* 53: 605–34.

Gill, J., and K.J. Meier. 2000. "Public administration research and practice: a methodological manifesto," *Journal of public administration research and theory* 10.1: 157–99.

Latham, G.P., and C.C. Pinder. 2005. "Work motivation theory and research at the dawn of the twenty-first century," *Annual review of psychology* 56: 485–516.

Latham, G.P., and E.A. Locke. 1991. "Self regulation through goal setting," *Organizational behavior and decision making process* 50: 212–47.

Latham, G.P., E.A. Locke, and N.E. Fassina. 2002. "The high performance cycle: standing the test of time," *The psychological management of individual performance: a handbook in the psychology of management in organizations.* S. Sonnentag, ed., 201–8. Hoboken, NJ: John Wiley & Sons, Inc.

Meier, K.J., and J.L. Brudney. 1997. *Applied statistics for public administration,* 4th ed. Orlando: Harcourt & Brace.

Sackett, P.R., R.M. Laczo, and Z.P. Lippe. 2003. "Differential prediction and the use of multiple predictors: the omitted variables problem," *Journal of applied psychology* 88.6: 1046–56.

Seijts, G.H., and G.P. Latham. 2000. "The effects of goal setting and group size on performance in a social dilemma," *Canadian journal of behavioral science* 32: 104–16.

Southworth, D.E. 2000. "Using statistical-based rating sheets to measure oral test inter-rater reliability," *Review of public personnel administration* 20.3: 43–57.

Stricker, L.S., D.A. Rock, and N.W. Burton. 1993. "Sex differences in predictions of college grades from Scholastic Aptitude Test scores," *Journal of educational psychology* 4: 710–18.

Vancouver, J.B., C.M. Thompson, and A.A. Williams. 2001. "The changing signs in the relationships among self-efficacy, personal goals, and performance," *Journal of applied psychology* 86: 605–20.

Wild, B.K., and B.A. Kerr. 1984. "Training adolescent job seekers in persuasion skills," *The vocational guidance quarterly* 33: 63–9.

Yeo, G.B., and A. Neal. 2004. "A multivariable analysis of effort, practice, and performance: effects of ability, conscientiousness, and goal orientation," *Journal of applied psychology* 89.2: 231–47.

Zohar, D., O. Tzischniski, and R. Epstein. 2003. "Effects of energy availability on immediate and delayed emotional reactions to work events," *Journal of applied psychology* 88.6: 1082–93.

CHAPTER 5

Blake, R.R., and J.S. Mouton. 1964. *The managerial grid.* Houston: Gulf.

Brief, A.P., and H.M. Weiss. 2002. "Organizational behavior: affect in the workplace," *Annual review of psychology* 53: 279–307.

Carnevale, P.J., and D.G. Pruitt. 1992. "Negotiation and mediation," *Annual review of psychology* 43: 531–82.

Chua, E.G., and W.B. Gudykunst. 1987. "Conflict resolution styles in low- and high-context cultures," *Communication research reports* 4.1: 32–37.

Hammock, G.S., D.R. Richardson, C.J. Pilkington, and M. Utley. 1990. "Measurement of conflict in social relationship," *Personality and individual differences* 11: 577–583.

Hersey, P., and K.H. Blanchard. 1988. *Management of organizational behavior: utilizing human resources*, 5th ed. Englewood Cliffs, NJ: Prentice Hall.

Ilgen, D.R., J.R. Hollenbeck, M. Johnson, and D. Jundt. 2004. "Teams in organizations: input-process-output models to IMOI models," *Annual review of psychology* 55: 517–43.

Kirkebride, P.S., S.F.Y. Tang, and R.I. Westwood. 1991. "Chinese conflict preferences and negotiating behaviors: cultural and psychological influences," *Organization studies* 12.3: 365–386.

McFarland, W.P., and W.H. Culp. 1992. "Interpersonal skill training for effective conflict resolution," *School counselor* 39.4: 304–310.

Mills, J., D. Robey, and L. Smith. 1985. "Conflict-handling and personality dimensions of project-management personnel," *Psychological reports* 57: 1135–1143.

Morrill, C., and C.K. Thomas. 1992. "Organizational conflict management as disputing process: the problem of social escalation," *Human communication research* 18: 400–428.

Putnam, L.L., and C.E. Wilson. 1982. "Communication strategies in organizational conflicts: reliability and validity of a measurement scale," *Communication Yearbook 6*. M. Burgoon, ed., 629–952. Beverly Hills: Sage.

Russell, J.A., J. Bachorowski, and J. Fernandez-Dols. 2003. "Facial and vocal expressions of emotion," *Annual review of psychology* 54: 329–49.

Southworth, D.E. 2000. "Using job performance as a component of civil service examinations," *Public personnel management* 29.3: 407–22.

Thomas, K.W., and R.H. Kilmann. 1974. *Thomas-Kilmann conflict MODE instrument.* Tuxedo, NY: Xicom.

Witteman, H. 1992. "Analyzing interpersonal conflict: nature of awareness, type of initiating event, situational perceptions, and management styles," *Western journal of communication* 56: 248–280.

CHAPTER 6

Bales, R.F., S.P. Cohen, and S.A. Williamson. 1979. *SYMLOG: a system for the multiple level observation of groups.* London: Collier.

Barley, S.R., and G. Kunda. 1992. "Design and devotion: surges of rational and normative ideologies of control in managerial discourse," *Administrative science quarterly* 37.3: 363–99.

Bouckaert, G. 1990. "The history of productivity," *Public productivity and management review* 14.1: 53–87.

Goffman, E. 1959. *The presentation of self in everyday life.* Garden City, NY: Doubleday.

Goffman, E. 1971. *Relations in public.* New York: Basic Books.

Littlejohn, S.W. *Theories of human communication*, 4th ed. Belmont, CA: Wadsworth.

Schlenker, B.R., and M.F. Weigold. 1992. "Interpersonal processes involving impression regulation and management," *Annual review of psychology* 43: 133–68.

U.S. Department of Labor. "Table B-1—employees on nonfarm payrolls by industry sector and selected industry detail." U.S. Department of Labor. Online at http://www.bls.gov (accessed November 4, 2008).

CHAPTER 7

Deutsch, M. 1975. "Equity, equality, need: what determines which value will be used as the basis of distributive justice, *Journal of social issues* 31: 137–50.

Ehrlich, P.R., and A.H. Ehrlich. 1991. *Healing the planet: Strategies for resolving the environmental crisis.* Reading, MA: Addison-Wesley.

The Equal Employment Opportunity Commission. "The Law." The Equal Employment Opportunity Commission. Online at www. eeoc.gov/abouteeoc/35th/thelaw/index.html (accessed September 27, 2008).

Fisicaro, S.A., and C.E. Lance. 1990. "Implications of three causal models for the measurement of halo effect," *Applied psychological measurement* 14: 419–29.

Herbert, D.A., and J.P. Katsulas. 1992. "The use and abuse of risk analysis in political debate," a paper presented to the American Forensic Association and the 1992 Speech Communication Association Convention, Chicago, Illinois.

HR-Guide.com. Chapter 3 Understanding test quality—concepts of reliability and validity. Online at www.hr-guide.com/data/G362.htm (accessed October 5, 2008)

Kahneman, D., and A. Tversky. 1979. "Prospect theory: an analysis of decision under risk," *Econometrica* 47: 263–91.

Levy, J.S. 1992. "An introduction to prospect theory," *Political Psychology* 13.2: 171–86.

Raskinski, K.A. 1987. "What's fair is fair—or is it? Value differences underlying public views about social justice," *Journal of personality and social psychology* 53.1: 201–11.

Southworth, D.E. 2006. "Fifteen years of using performance assessment as a component of civil service examinations," a paper presented at the 2006 National Conference of the American Society for Public Administration, Denver, Colorado.

Wilson, M., and W.C. Wang. 1995. "Complex composites: issues that arise in combining different modes of assessment," *Applied psychological measurement* 19: 51–71.

CHAPTER 8

Bies, R.J., and D.L. Shapiro. 1987. "Interactional fairness judgments: the influence of causal accounts," *Social justice research* 1: 199–218.

Bobocel, D.R., E. Agar, J.P. Meyer, and P.G. Irving. 1998. "Managerial accounts and fairness perceptions in conflict resolution: differentiating the effect of minimizing responsibility and providing justification," *Basic applied social psychology* 20: 133–43.

Cacioppo, J.T., and W.L. Gardner. 1999. "Emotion," *Annual review of psychology* 50: 191–214.

Diener, E., S. Oishi, and R.E. Lucas. 2003. "Personality, culture and subjective well-being: emotional and cognitive evaluations of life," *Annual review of psychology* 54: 403–26.

Diener, E., and R.E. Lucas. 1999. "Personality and subjective well being," *Well-being: the foundations of hedonic psychology.* D. Kahneman, E. Deiner, and N. Schwartz, eds. New York: Russell Sage Foundation.

Edwards, W., and B. Fasolo. 2001. "Decision technology," *Annual review of psychology* 52: 581–606.

Fischhoff, B., S. Lichtenstein, S. Slovic, S.C. Derby, and R.L. Keeney. 1981. *Acceptable risk*. Cambridge: Cambridge University Press.

Fiske, A.P. 1992. "The four elements of sociality: framework for a unified theory of social relations," *Psychological review* 99: 689–723.

Kahle, L.R. 1983. *Social values and social change: adaptations to life in America*. New York: Praeger.

Kamakura, W.A., and T.P. Novak. 1992. "Value-system segmentation: exploring the meaning of LOV," *Journal of consumer research* 19.6: 119–32.

Lickona, T. 2004. "Why character matters." Online at http://www. maxwell.syr.edu/plegal/ ppac/ch11.html (accessed October 5, 2008)

March, J.G. 1994. *A primer for decision making*. New York: Free Press.

Markman, A.B., and D. Gentner. 2001. "Thinking," *Annual review of psychology* 52: 223–47.

Mellers, B.A., A. Schwartz, and A.D.J. Cooke. 1998. "Judgment and decision making," *Annual review of psychology* 49: 447–77.

Miller, D.T. 2001. "Disrespect and the experience of injustice," *Annual review of psychology* 52: 527–53.

Petty, R.E., D.T. Wegener, and L.R. Fabrigar. 1997. "Attitudes and attitude change," *Annual review of psychology* 48: 609–47.

Rokeach, M. 1967. *Value survey*. Palo Alto, CA: Consulting Psychologists Press.

Rokeach, M., and S.J. Ball-Rokeach. 1989. "Stability and change in American value priorities," *American psychologist* 44.5: 775–84.

Ryan, R.M., and E.L. Deci. 2001. "On happiness and human potential: a review of research on hedonic and eudaimonic well-being," *Annual review of psychology* 52: 141–66.

Shafir, E., and R.A. LeBoeuf. 2002. "Rationality," *Annual review of psychology* 53: 491–517.

Shapiro, D.L., E.H. Buttner, and B. Barry. 1994. "Explanations for rejection decisions: what factors enhance their perceived adequacy and moderate their enhancement of justice perceptions," *Organizational behavior and human decision processes* 58: 346–68.

Victor, B., and J.B. Cullen. 1988. "The organizational bases of ethical work climates," *Administrative science quarterly* 33 (March): 101–25.

Waterman, A.S. 1993. "Two conceptions of happiness: contrasts of personal expressiveness (eudaimonia) and hedonic enjoyment," *Journal of personality and social psychology* 64: 678–91.

Index

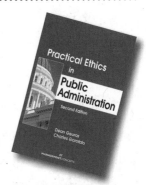

Introducing... The Practical Leader Series!

Offering a roadmap to achieving leadership effectiveness in today's complex world, each book in this series explores a different essential element of successful leadership. This series provides insightful, real-world perspectives, as well as practical tools and techniques to help readers maximize their potential—personally and professionally.

BONUS! Each book comes with a CD-ROM offering additional tools, techniques, exercises, and other resources to help readers become effective leaders.

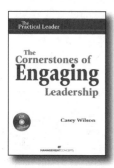

The Cornerstones of Engaging Leadership
Casey Wilson

The Cornerstones of Engaging Leadership connects what we know about engagement on an organizational level to what an individual leader can do to increase engagement. Using real-world examples, author Casey Wilson reveals the key actions leaders must take to connect with and engage others—build trust, leverage unique motivators, manage performance from a people-centric perspective, and engage emotions. By committing to these four cornerstones of engaging leadership, leaders can unleash the potential of others and inspire effective performance.

ISBN 978-1-56726-218-6 ■ Product Code B186 ■ 151 pages

The Five Commitments of a Leader
Mark Leheney

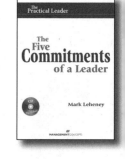

In *The Five Commitments of a Leader*, author Mark Leheney presents a revealing way to examine leadership—through the commitments a leader makes (or fails to make). He focuses on five commitments a leader must make to be effective—commitments to the self, people, the organization, the truth, and leadership. Leheney challenges leaders to understand stated versus actual commitments, and through self-assessment and practice tools, he encourages leaders to ask themselves accountability-creating questions.

ISBN 978-1-56726-219-3 ■ Product Code B193 ■ 160 pages

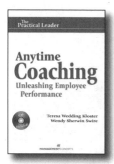

Anytime Coaching: Unleashing Employee Performance
Teresa Wedding Kloster and Wendy Sherwin Swire

Anytime Coaching: Unleashing Employee Performance is a practical guide to putting coaching skills to use at any time. Learning from real-life stories, simple tips and techniques, and the Anytime Coaching model, managers ranging from first-time supervisors to senior executives will be equipped with a set of coaching tools they can use immediately to transform the way they work with employees and colleagues—unleashing their best thinking and growing their overall competence.

ISBN 978-1-56726-237-7 ■ Product Code B377 ■ 186 pages

Order today for a 30-day risk-free trial!
Visit **www.managementconcepts.com/pubs** or call **703-790-9595**